INTRODUCTION TO INDIAN PHILOSOPHY

INTRODUCTION TO INDIAN PHILOSOPHY

JWALA PRASAD

FOREWORD

R. D. RANADE

GYAN

Published by

Gyan Publishing House
5, Ansari Road
Daryaganj, New Delhi-110002
Phone: 011-47034999, 9811692060
E-mail: books@gyanbooks.com

Distribution Network
gyanbooks.com
India, USA, Canada, UK, Australia

ISBN: 978-93-6780-098-0 (PB)

First Published, 1928

2nd Impression 2024

Printed at: Gyan Press, Delhi.

INTRODUCTION TO INDIAN PHILOSOPHY
Author: JWALA PRASAD

Introduction to Indian Philosophy

BY

JWALA PRASAD, M.A.

Assistant Professor of Philosophy, Robertson College, Jubbulpore (the Central Provinces)

WITH

A FOREWORD

BY

R. D. RANADE, M.A.

Professor of Philosophy, Allahabad University

ALLAHABAD

THE INDIAN PRESS, LTD.

1928

Printed by K. Mittra at The Indian Press, Ltd., Allahabad.

FOREWORD

Prof. Jwala Prasad, M.A., of Robertson College, Jubbulpore, has laid the student-world under deep obligation by writing a concise and trenchant account of Indian philosophy, which, as is now well-known, most of the Indian universities have prescribed in their B.A. curriculum, so that the students might make a comparative study of Indian philosophy along with that of Western philosophers. The volumes written on Indian philosophy by Professors Radhakrishnan, Das Gupta, Belwalkar and the rest, are meant more for scholars, who want to carry on their researches in the higher fields of Indian philosophy. Thus, at most, they could be used as reference books by those who are making their first acquaintance with Indian philosophy at the B.A. The B.A. students of Indian universities who want to take a pass degree in Indian philosophy have not the patience or the leisure to study these great works. For them, what is wanted is a concise statement of the whole subject which would enable them to refresh their memories, and which would create an intelligent interest in them for further studies. There are very few concise manuals of Indian philosophy of this kind. Prof. Jwala Prasad has done great service in writing a book which might be regarded as probably the most suitable introduction among these to this difficult subject.

Within the short compass at his disposal, Prof. Jwala Prasad has done his work ably. He touches even the most difficult points in these systems, and treats them in a concise manner. His account of Jainism, Buddhism, and Nyāya might be regarded as instances in point. We could have wished that the account which the author gives of the Vedāntic systems was more detailed. But let us hope that Prof. Jwala Prasad will remedy this in a later edition of his book. We are indeed glad to see that Prof. Jwala Prasad is going to England for further studies in Indian philosophy, and are also glad that he would be taking up there for his research work the subject of "Indian Epistemology," which he has been cherishing for a long time past, and upon which there are very few standard treatises. Let us hope that Prof. Jwala Prasad's work would be a distinct contribution to this subject, especially as he knows the texts of Indian philosophy at first hand, is fully conversant with the methods of European philosophy, and will be under the training of the great savants of philosophy in the West. We wish him a happy and prosperous career, and we also wish that Prof. Jwala Prasad on his return would be able to incorporate parts of his research work on Indian Epistemology in his second edition of the present work.

The Glossary of terms in Indian Philosophy, as well as the Bibliography of works on Indian Philosophy, which Prof. Jwala Prasad gives towards the end of this book, will be found highly useful by the students.

University of Allahabad,
31st August, 1928. R. D. RANADE.

THE AUTHOR'S PREFACE

The following pages have been written to fill up a real gap in the literature of the subject with which they deal. It is true that some quite good books on Indian Philosophy have appeared recently in English, but none of them, so far as I know, satisfactorily caters for the needs of a beginner in the subject, or is as handy, intelligible and yet comprehensive as the average reader would desire it to be. Most of the sections contained in this treatise originally appeared as articles in the *Nerbadda*—a college magazine, and the idea of expanding them, with the necessary additions and alterations, into a book first occurred to me when I came across some of the volumes of the 'World's Manuals' of the Oxford University Press. Later on, some of my friends and colleagues also suggested the need of a similar work, and now, when it is ready, I believe it will serve the purpose for which it has been designed.

Consistently with the aim of this publication the various chapters are calculated to provide a clear and brief exposition of the subject with which they deal, and an effort has been made to keep the matter and the form as close to the original sources as possible. Indian Philosophy is peculiarly rich in definitions and classifications, and hence the language becomes profusely technical. I have tried to reduce technicality to a minimum, although it has to be recognised that it cannot be dispensed with altogether, for the use of suitable technical terms often goes a great way towards securing accuracy of thought and brevity of exposition.

I am indebted to a number of writers, both old and new, for some of the valuable material contained in this book, and a list of the important works which I have consulted is given at the end.

My most sincere thanks are due to Professor W. S. Rowlands of our own college, who has very carefully gone through the whole work, and has offered valuable suggestions before its publication in the present form.

To Professor R. D. Ranade of the Allahabad University I am deeply obliged for having read the book in manuscript and written a Foreword to the same.

JUBBULPORE,
22nd August, 1928. J. P.

CONTENTS

GENERAL INTRODUCTION.

GENERAL INTRODUCTION.

"The genius of the East, led by India, has always gravitated towards speculation in Metaphysics. India, for ever prying behind the veil of the Unknowable, busied herself with the why of the phenomenal universe, and finding the problem insoluble named it Māyā and confined herself to the Absolute. The West, 'seeing God in clouds and hearing Him in the wind,' sought out the path to the absolute by dragging her secrets from Nature, and having discovered some of the mysteries of the phenomenal world she applied her knowledge to practical matters . . . ." So says Mr. Stanley Rice in a recent work—*The Challenge of Asia.* Although, to my mind, the quotation does not express the whole truth about the thought and life of the East, yet it brings out remarkably the most outstanding feature of the general mentality of the people of that part of our globe. Even now, in his own way, the Indian is a philosopher and religious man first and anything else afterwards. It was in his country that the mystic Aryan poets of yore sang their charming philosophy of the earth and the heavens through the glorious hymns of the Vedas and the pious teachers of spirituality imparted their instruction through the remarkable dialogues of the Upaniṣads. It was in India that acute dialecticians like Gautama and Kaṇāda evolved that peculiarly Indian aphoristic form of literature which is known as the Sūtras, and the various sections of her people, imbued with an indomitable burning fervour for their own sects and systems of religion and philosophy, constantly arrayed themselves in contending parties and offered to one another the toughest intellectual fights that the world has ever witnessed in the history of human thought. And now, in the present day, it is again in this same land that a new era in the cultural progress of mankind has set in by the coming together of the peoples of the East and the West. The intellectual and the political needs of both the Eastern and the Western nations naturally require that they should try to understand one another as closely and extensively as possible, and I am confident that an effort to study Indian Thought in its varied phases and at the various stages of development must be a very substantial step towards the achievement of this goal.

To those who are acquainted with Western Philosophy a study of the various systems of Indian Thought will reveal striking similarities between some of the thinkers of India and those of the West. The Indian syllogism in the Nyāya and the Categories of the Vaiśeṣika naturally remind us of the Syllogism and the Categories in the system of Aristotle. The doctrine of Transmigration and the Immortality of the Soul, so strongly advocated in all the schools of Indian Philosophy save one, at once takes us back to such Western thinkers as Plato and Pythagoras. The Brahman Absolute of Śaṁkara's Vedānta makes us think of the Idealism of Hegel, and the modified Monism of Rāmānuja presents a close affinity to the philosophy of Spinoza. The doctrine that *esse* is *percipi*, so familiar to Western readers in the philosophy of Berkeley, is discovered with surprise to have already existed in the Idealism of the Vedānta. The Realistic and the Idealistic Schools of Buddhism represent almost all the main shades of European Thought, and the doctrine of the 'nigodas' in Jainism reveals a remarkable resemblance to the 'monads' of Leibnitz.

Besides noticing these similarities, an acute observer cannot help discovering the existence of important cultural influences which have recently affected the life and literature of both the East and the West. The interpretation of Buddha and Buddhism by such Europeans as the author of *The Light of Asia* and the representation of Hinduism and its philosophy through the efforts of such European and Indian enthusiasts as the founders and the followers of Theosophy, have exercised a wonderful influence over the peoples of the West and have contributed immensely towards the creating of that new civilisation which represents a remarkable blending of the two cultures, which at first appeared so divergent and uncompromising.

To come to a very recent development in the political life of India, it must be interesting to see how the doctrine of passive resistance or non-violence, known as the Non-Co-operation Movement led by Mahātmā Gāndhi, ultimately owes its origin to the principle of 'ahiṁsā' (harmlessness), which is so much emphasised in almost all the systems of Indian Philosophy, especially in the Yoga and Buddhism. '*Ahiṁsā paramo dharmaḥ*'—'Harmlessness is the highest virtue'—is a maxim on the lips of every Hindu, Jaina and Buddhist. It may be pointed out, however, that this application of the doctrine of harmlessness, which was originally directed to the end of obtaining spiritual emancipation, to the field of politics, with a view to suggesting a means of securing political freedom, is altogether a new departure in the history of India, and I am sure it cannot be shown to be in accord with any of the political theories or traditions that have guided the political conduct of her people in the past. I am not sure whether those who have been responsible for the introduction of this principle into the political life of

India are conscious of this or not, but one thing is evident, that the wonderful sway which the new political creed held over the majority of Indians for some time was mostly due to this association of it with one of the most favourite doctrines of Indian Philosophy and Theology.

The ultimate beginnings of philosophical speculation are not to be found in books, but in the musings of a thinker, which first find expression in private conversation, then in public discourses and discussions, and finally in written treatises. The origin of Indian Philosophy is not to be traced to the earliest works that we can get at, for example, the Vedas, but to those primitive efforts of our ancestors at thinking which perhaps all the Aryan races, both European and Asiatic, can claim as their common heritage. The results of this early speculation must have been first handed down from one generation to another in the form of a growing philosophical tradition, and then they must have found a place in what we have come to know as the sacred scriptures. Later on, they began to be separated from these religious treatises and developed gradually into the form of a philosophical literature. This explanation of the origin of philosophical thinking in general and of the beginnings of Indian Philosophy in particular is not a mere guess, for it is clearly borne out by the nature of our own individual and what we may call our academic efforts at reflection, and by the dialogues which were so prominent a feature of philosophical exposition in India and also of the writings of the ancient philosophers of the West. Any one who is acquainted with the Socratic and the Platonic methods or the Upaniṣadic dialogues, knows the truth of this assertion too well to require any further elucidation. The original foundations of the various philosophical systems in India are to be found in a speculative tradition which took its rise in and was handed down by the families of various teachers—the 'gurukulas,' as they were called. And as it is quite conceivable that there should have been a good number of these 'gurukulas' with their own philosophical traditions, and that a considerable time must have elapsed before these could have been recorded in writing, it is no wonder that the earliest written literature which is available to us already displays a remarkable diversity and general advance of philosophical thought. For example, in the Ṛigveda, which is the oldest book available in Indian literature, we find quite an advanced stage of speculation, and considering the contents of all the four Vedas together, we can safely assert that the germs of all the orthodox systems of Indian Philosophy are already present in them, and it is in fact upon the basis of this diverse kind of material that the later structure of Indian philosophical thought is built.

The systems in Indian Philosophy may be classified under two broad heads: Firstly, those which directly or indirectly depend for their origin and proof upon the religious scriptures, which are either the Vedas themselves or based upon the Vedas. These may be called the Orthodox Systems, and consist of the well-known Six Schools of Hindu Philosophy, *viz.* : I. The Nyāya ; II. The Vaiśeṣika ; III. The Sāṁkhya ; IV. The Yoga ; V. The Pūrva Mīmāṁsā ; VI. The Uttara Mīmāṁsā or the Vedānta. These Orthodox Systems derive their inspiration from, and depend greatly for their proof upon, what are known technically as 'Śruti,' 'Smṛiti,' and the 'Purāṇas.' The 'Śruti' denotes the four Vedas, the Brāhmaṇas, the Āraṇyakas and the Upaniṣads. The term 'Smṛiti' means the Codes of Law, the Bhagavadgītā, the Rāmāyaṇa and the Mahābhārata. By the 'Purāṇas' we understand the semi-mythological, semi-historical literature, the major portion of which is supposed to be of a comparatively much later date. Secondly, there are a few systems which altogether deny the authority of the Vedic scriptures, and may, therefore, be called the Heterodox Systems. The chief of these are Materialism, Jainism, and Buddhism. They are based upon the teachings of Chārvāka and Bṛihaspati, Mahāvīra and Gautama Buddha respectively. Besides these, there are some minor schools under both heads, which are, directly or indirectly, the offshoots of the main systems. It is difficult to determine exactly the chronological order of the various systems of Indian Philosophy. The following, however, would be a fairly correct arrangement for purposes of exposition, and the same we shall adopt in this book: I. The Philosophy of the Vedic Period; II. The Philosophy of the Epic Period; III. The Philosophy of the Heterodox Schools; IV. The Six Schools of the Hindu Philosophy.

I. THE PHILOSOPHY OF THE VEDIC PERIOD.

I. THE PHILOSOPHY OF THE VEDIC PERIOD.

1. The Four Vedas or the Saṁhitās.

The Vedas are the earliest records of human thought so far available to us. In the words of Professor Max Müller, 'they are to us unique and priceless guides in opening before our eyes tombs of thought richer in relics than the royal tombs of Egypt, and more ancient and primitive in thought than the oldest hymns of Babylonian or Arcadian poets.' There are four Vedas, called the Saṁhitās (collections), namely, the Ṛigveda, the Sāmaveda, the Yajurveda, and the Atharvaveda. The word 'veda' is derived from the Sanskṛit root 'vid'—'to know'—and means 'knowledge.' The Vedas have always been looked upon by the Hindus as the original source of all enlightenment, the embryonic beginnings of all science and literature—nay, the very manifestation of the Supreme Spirit (Brahman) in the form of Logos. According to the orthodox opinion, they are divine and eternal, and consequently possess the highest, and an altogether indisputable authority. However, all scholars now agree that these collections of hymns were compiled at different periods during the course of the development of the Indo-Aryan civilisation in its earlier stages, and that the Ṛigveda is by far the oldest and the most important of them. The dates assigned to this compilation by different scholars range between 6000 B.C. and 1200 B.C. The late Paṇḍit Bāl Gaṅgādhar Tilak put it at about 4000 B.C. According to Professors Max Müller and Macdonell, 1200 B.C. is the most probable period during which the work was compiled. In the absence of historical records or any other source of evidence, the date of the compilation of the Vedas is more or less a matter of surmise, although there are sufficient reasons to believe that the date of the Ṛigveda cannot be later than 1200 B.C. The Sāma and the Yajur Vedas, which were compiled at a later date, are not very different from the Ṛigveda. The former contains a selection of hymns from the Ṛigveda, which were meant to be sung according to certain fixed melodies, and the latter also contains verses of the same Veda arranged in the order in which they were to be recited during the performance of sacrifices. Besides the verses taken from the Ṛigveda, the Yajurveda also contains a number of original prose formulas. The Atharvaveda belongs to a much later date and represents a type of thought and religion very different from that of the Ṛigveda. The religion of the Atharva is comparatively inferior to that of the Ṛigveda, being full of all kinds of superstitions and baser forms of worship, which present so great a contrast to the loftier ideals of religious life and higher conceptions of Godhood contained in the Ṛigveda. For a philosophical survey of the Vedic period we have naturally to turn to the hymns of the Ṛigveda, or the same as found in the Yajurveda.

2. The Philosophy of the Vedas.

The hymns of the Ṛigveda represent the most spontaneous expression of the burning curiosity of the primitive Aryan mind aroused by the extremely novel and wonderful surroundings in which it must have found itself when the Aryans entered and settled down, first in the beautiful plains of the Punjab, and subsequently in the fertile regions watered by the Ganges and the Jumna. The verses represent hymns to a number of gods and goddesses who personify the main forces of nature, and the terms in which they are eulogised indicate the religious and philosophic conceptions of their authors. If, as Plato said, philosophy begins in wonder, in some of the Vedic hymns we find the most characteristic examples of an early philosophical striving on the part of the human mind. A careful study of the Ṛigveda will show that while individual gods are adored and the various phenomena of nature are attributed to them, the need of finding one comprehensive unity amid all diversity and one fundamental cause for all the manifold causes and effects is constantly pressing itself upon these poet philosophers of yore, and that as a result of this we already find in the Ṛigveda the theistic, the pantheistic and the monistic tendencies in juxtaposition with the more usual and predominant polytheistic notions. We can do no better than quote some of the important hymns to illustrate this characteristic of the Vedic philosophy and religion. The following extract from the Hymn of Creation (Ṛigveda, X. 129) is a beautiful example of early philosophical inquisitiveness:

1. Then there was neither being nor not-being.
The atmosphere was not, nor sky above it.
What covered all? and where? by what protected?
Was there the fathomless abyss of waters?

* * *

6. Who is it knows? Who here can tell us surely
From what and how this universe has risen?
And whether not till after it the gods lived?
Who then can know from what it has arisen?

7. The source from which this universe has risen,
And whether it was made, or uncreated,
He only knows, who from the highest heaven
Rules, the all-seeing Lord—or does not He know?

(From the Ṛigveda by Kaegi.)

Again the following, called by Professor Max Müller the Hymn to the Unknown God, which is repeated so usually by the Hindus as a prayer, is a fine expression of the eagerness of the Aryan mind to get at the conception of the highest deity:

1. In the beginning there arose the germ of golden light, Hiraṇyagarbha; he was the one born lord of all that is. He established the earth and this sky—Who is the god to whom we should offer our sacrifice?

2. He who gives life, he who gives strength; whose command all the bright gods revere; whose shadow is immortality and mortality (gods and men)—Who is the god to whom we should offer our sacrifice?

3. He through his power became the sole king of this breathing and slumbering world—he who governs all, man and beast—Who is the god to whom we should offer our sacrifice?

4. He through whose greatness these snowy mountains are, and the sea, they say, with the Rasa, the distant river, he whose two arms these regions are—Who is the god to whom we should offer our sacrifice?

5. He through whom the sky is strong, and the earth firm, he through whom the heaven was established, nay the highest heaven, he who measured the light in the

air—Who is the god to whom we should offer our sacrifice?

* * *

Then follows the verse as if in answer to the question at the end of each of the above stanzas:

'O Prajāpati, no other but thou hast held together all these things; whatever we desire in sacrificing to thee, may that be ours, may we be the lords of wealth.'

As Professor Max Müller says, 'with this conception of Prajāpati as the lord of all created things and as the supreme deity, the monotheistic yearning was satisfied, even though the existence of other gods was not denied.'

The following verses as containing the germs of a monotheistic religion and a monistic philosophy will be found interesting:

'The sages call that one in many ways, they call it Agni, Yama, Mātariśvan.' (R. V., I. 164—46.)

'That One breathed breathlessly by itself, other than that there nothing since has been.' (R. V., X. 129—2.)

The doctrine of 'ātman' (self) and 'karman' (action) is present in the Ṛigveda, although not in the form in which it is to be found in the later Vedic literature—the Brāhmaṇas, the Āraṇyakas and the Upaniṣads. There are hymns which indicate that the soul is supposed to be distinct from the body and separable from it during intervals of unconsciousness and after death. Further, it is recognised that the soul of a man is subject to suffering and enjoyment in the other world according to the nature of the deeds during his lifetime.

3. The Brāhmaṇas, the Āraṇyakas and the Upaniṣads.

The Vedic literature consists of the Vedas, the Brāhmaṇas, the Āraṇyakas and the Upaniṣads. The

Śrauta and the Smārta or the Gṛihya Sūtras also form part of the Vedic lore. The Brāhmaṇas are written in prose and for the most part explain the meaning and application of the Vedic hymns with reference to the performance of sacrifices. The word 'Brāhmaṇa' means 'that which is related to prayer' (brahman). We find in the Brāhmaṇas, as Professor Weber says, 'the oldest rituals we have, the oldest linguistic explanations, the oldest traditional narratives and the oldest philosophical speculations . . . With regard to age they all date from the period of the transition from Vedic civilisation and culture to the Brāhmaṇic mode of thought and social order. Nay, they help to bring about this very transition, and some of them belong rather to the time of its commencement, others rather to that of its termination.' Each of the four Vedas has its own Brāhmaṇas and they differ from one another according to the subject-matter of the Veda to which each of them is attached. The chief Brāhmaṇas are the Aitareya and the Śatapatha, which belong to the Ṛig and the Yajur Vedas respectively. The following quotation from the Śatapatha would show how the germs of the later Vedāntic doctrine of Brahman and that of Name and Form, which we find also in Buddhism, can be traced back to this period:

"Verily in the beginning this (universe) was the Brahman (neuter). It created the gods; and having created the gods, it made them ascend these worlds: Agni this terrestrial world, Vāyu the air and Sūrya the sky . . . Then the Brahman itself went up to the sphere beyond. Having gone up to the sphere beyond, it considered: 'How can I descend again into these worlds?' It then descended again by means of these two—Form and Name. Whatever has a name, that is name; and that again which has no name and which one knows by its form, 'this is (of a certain) form,' that is form: as far as there are Form and Name so far, indeed, extends this (universe). These indeed are the two great forces of Brahman; and, verily, he who knows the two great forces of Brahman becomes himself a great force." (Eggeling's Translation—S.B.E., XLIV.)

The Āraṇyakas or 'Forest Treatises' and the Upaniṣads—'Confidential Talks'—form appendices to the Brāhmaṇas and represent a progressive transition from ritualism to abstract thought. The Āraṇyakas, as the name signifies, were meant for those who retired from the worldly life of action and devoted themselves to meditation. The philosophy of the Āraṇyakas is very much allied to that of the Upaniṣads, and this we shall notice in the next section.

4. The Philosophy of the Upaniṣads.

The Upaniṣads mark the beginnings of pure philosophical speculation in the history of Indian thought. Most of the Vedic verses are primarily hymns to the various deities and the philosophical implications are only to be deduced from their contents. The authors of the hymns have a more practical than a theoretical interest, and the standpoint of their enquiry is mostly objective. However, on the whole, in the Vedas we find ritualism and philosophy mixed together, and while the Brāhmaṇas are a further development mainly of the ritualistic aspect of the Vedas, the Āraṇyakas and the Upaniṣads primarily represent an advance in the philosophical implications of the same. As we pass from the Vedas to the Upaniṣads the speculation becomes primarily subjective. The nature of 'self' is the main theme of the Upaniṣadic philosophy, and knowledge of the self is discovered to be the key to the mystery of the whole universe. 'What is that,' asks the philosopher in the Muṇḍaka Upaniṣad, 'which being known, everything else becomes known?' (Muṇḍ., I. 1. 3.) The Upaniṣads not only expound the philosophy of the self, but also emphasise the importance of the life of meditation as against the life of ritualism. In the Chāndogya Upaniṣad we find that the value of 'inner sacrifice' (meditation) is shown to be higher than that of the 'formal sacrifice' (the actual performance of it). It is said that 'our real sacrifice consists in making oblations to the Prāṇa (breath) within us. One who has not known this inner sacrifice, even if he goes in for formal sacrifice, throws oblations merely on ashes. On the other hand, he who knows this inner sacrifice is relieved of his sins as surely as wool is burnt in a flame of fire. Knowing this inner sacrifice, even if a man were to do acts of charity for a Cāṇḍāla, he would verily be regarded as having sacrificed to the Universal Soul.' (Chānd., V. 19—24.) Again, the Kauṣītaki Upaniṣad tells us that 'the ancient sages did not go in for formal sacrifice knowing that an endless sacrifice was going on all the while within their selves.' (Kauṣ., II. 5.)

Altogether there are about one hundred and twelve Upaniṣads, although the more important of these are only thirteen or fourteen in number. The Upaniṣadic period extends from 1200 B.C. to about 500 B.C., and the Upaniṣads may be assigned, as Professor Paul Deussen assigns them, to four successive periods :—

(1) *The Ancient Prose Upaniṣads*—Bṛihad-āraṇyaka, Chāndogya, Taittirīya, Aitareya, Kauṣītaki and Kena.

(2) *The Metrical Upaniṣads*—Kaṭhaka, Īśa, Śvetāśvatara, Muṇḍaka and Mahānārāyaṇa.
(3) *The Later Prose Upaniṣads*—Praśna, Maitrāyaṇīya and Māṇḍukya.
(4) *The Later Atharva Upaniṣads*—These were a number of later and minor theological treatises written after the style of the Upaniṣads, and came to be attached to the Atharvaveda; for example, Atharvaśiras, Nīlarudra, Brahmavidyā, Dhyānabindu, etc., which dealt with a variety of subjects.

The Chāndogya and the Bṛihadāraṇyaka are the earliest and the most important of the Upaniṣads and it is mostly their texts that form the basis of the exposition of the doctrines of the later schools of Indian Philosophy, especially those of the Vedānta. The Brahmasūtras of Bādarāyaṇa, also known as the Vedānta Sūtras, and the commentaries thereon, are full of references to the texts of these ancient prose Upaniṣads. The origin of the Sāṁkhya and the Yoga doctrines also can, in several cases, be traced to some of these Upaniṣads. The term 'vedānta' (literally 'the end of the Vedas') has also been applied as a general title to the whole Upaniṣadic literature, for the Upaniṣads form the last portion of the Vedas.

The philosophy of the Upaniṣads may be discussed under a number of heads, but for the most part there is one conception which dominates the whole of Upaniṣadic thought, *viz.*, that there is ultimately only one principle of reality, and it is Brahman or the universal self. All diversity and plurality of existence is either an illusion altogether or a manifestation of this same principle in a variety of forms. These two explanations of the phenomenal world form the basis of the two later schools of the Vedānta—the monism (*advaita*) of Śaṁkarācārya and the modified monism (*viśiṣṭādvaita*) of Rāmānuja. The following texts are typical expressions of the pervading note of the Upaniṣadic philosophy :—

(i) 'Verily this whole is Brahman' (*sarvam khalu idam Brahma*).

(ii) 'Brahman is the self within us' (*eṣa ma ātmā antar hṛidaye*)—Chānd., 3—14.

(iii) 'Truly Brahman is this self (ātman)' (*ayam ātmā Brahma*)—Bṛih., 44-5.

(iv) 'Thou art that' (*tat tvam asi*)—Chānd., 6, 8-7.

(v) 'I am Brahman' (*aham Brahma asmi*)—Bṛin., 1. 4—10.

In the first of the above texts the whole universe is identified with Brahman, and the rest of them emphasise the identity of the individual self with the universal self. As a corollary of this monistic doctrine, follows the principle that the knowledge of Brahman is a key to the knowledge of everything in the universe. 'Verily he who has seen, heard and comprehended and known the self, by him is this entire universe known,' says the Bṛihadāraṇyaka (2. 4-5). Then again, the Chāndogya —'Dost thou then ask for that instruction, by which the unheard becomes (already) heard, the uncomprehended comprehended, the unknown known? What then, most noble sir, is this instruction?' 'Just as, my dear sir, from a lump of clay everything that consists of clay is known, the change is a matter of words alone, a mere name, it is in reality only clay,—thus my dear sir, is this instruction.'

In the words of Professor Deussen, 'here the manifold change of the one substance is explained as a mere word-play, mere name, exactly as Parmenides asserts that all which men regard as real is mere name.' In the following text of the Bṛihadāraṇyaka the very existence of plurality is denied:

> 'In the spirit should this be perceived,
> Here there is no plurality anywhere,
> From death to death again he rushes blindly,
> Who fancies that he here sees difference.'

That Brahman is the all-comprehensive cosmic principle is clearly expressed in the following passage from the Bṛihadāraṇyaka (2. 4—10): 'Just as, when a fire is laid with damp wood, clouds of smoke spread all around, so in truth from this great being have been breathed forth the Ṛigveda, the Yajurveda, the Sāmaveda, the hymns of the Atharvans and the Aṅgirasas, the narratives, the histories, the sciences, the mystical doctrines (Upaniṣads), the poems, the proverbs, the parables and expositions—all these have been breathed forth from him.'

It is to be noted, however, that the Upaniṣadic doctrine is not always necessarily monistic or pantheistic. There are to be found a few texts which have clear dualistic implications either with regard to the distinction of the individual and the universal spirit or the recognition of matter side by side with spirits. Such texts have always been regarded as lending support to the theistic schools of the Nyāya and the Vaiśeṣika, and the dualistic doctrine of the Sāṁkhya. 'That is full and this is full. From that full rises this full. Taking away this full from that, what remains is yet full,' says the Upaniṣad, the meaning of the text being that although the universe arises out of Brahman it does not exhaust its fulness, or in other words, Brahman transcends the universe. This view is definitely opposed to pantheism, which identifies God with the universe and denies transcendence. The following verses from the Śvetāśvatara (4. 6-7) bring out remarkably the distinction between the individual and the divine spirit:

> Two fair-plumaged close friends
> Surround one and the same tree;
> One of them tastes the sweet berries,
> The other, without eating, only gazes downwards.
>
> To such a tree the spirit sunk down
> In its impotence mourns, a prey to delusion,
> Yet when it worships and beholds of the other
> The omnipotence and majesty, then its grief departs.

All the scholars agree that the following verse anticipates the Sāṁkhya doctrine of the three qualities (*guṇas*) of matter (*prakṛiti*), and also expresses the usual two kinds of relations that exist between the individual spirits and matter:—

> 'The one she-goat, red and white and blackish,
> Casts many young, who are fashioned like her ;
> The one ram leaps on her in the ardour of love,
> The other ram abandons her, his companion.'
>
> (Śvetāśvatara, 4-5.)

Here matter with its threefold qualities of 'goodness' (*sattva*), passion (*rajas*), and darkness (*tamas*), as these have been expounded in the Sāṁkhya, has been compared to a she-goat of three colours, white, red and black, corresponding to those three qualities respectively. The two kinds of rams represent two kinds of spirits, *viz.*, those that become attached to the pleasure of the material world and those that abandon them. The comparison of the three qualities of matter to the three colours is thus explained by a commentator: "In this verse by the words 'red' and 'white' and 'black' are to be understood *rajas*, *sattva*, and *tamas*. The red is *rajas* (passion), because it naturally makes (things) red, that is to say, it puts them into agitation; the white is *sattvam* (goodness), because it naturally makes (things) bright; the black is *tamas* (*darkness*), because it naturally makes (things) 'dark.' "

According to the Upaniṣads, emancipation or salvation consists in attaining the knowledge of Brahman. It is a 'consciousness of unity with the ātman as first principle of all things. It is essentially, on the one hand, an annihilation of all desire, and on the other, an annihilation of the illusion of a manifold universe.' The achievement of this end requires a life of strict discipline—the practice of *yoga* (concentration), and the Yoga philosophy has its beginnings in this need of human life.

'When every passion vanishes,
That finds a home in the human heart,
Then he who is mortal becomes immortal,
Here already he has attained Brahman.'

It may be noted that according to the Upaniṣads the soul is always pure—even when it is confined in the individual body, and emancipation, which is really self-realisation, only means a consciousness of this intrinsic purity of the soul and its identity with the universal soul after the removal of illusion due to false knowledge.

All souls are originally
Free from darkness and without stain,
'Already awakened and delivered before the world was,
They rise up,' saith the Master.

(Chāndogya, 8. 3-2.)

Our exposition of the Upaniṣadic doctrine of Brahman would be incomplete if we omitted to mention that according to the Upaniṣads this absolute is to be described only negatively, for it is the pure subject and therefore beyond all the categories of objective experience. Self-realisation is a peculiar immediate experience in which the distinction of the subject and the object disappears altogether. The ultimate subject can never become the object. The following texts of the Upaniṣads would be of interest in this connection:

> 'From which all speech with the mind turns away unable to reach it.' —Taittirīya, ii. 4.
>
> 'The eye does not go thither, nor speech nor mind. We do not know. We do not understand how any one can teach it.' —Kena, ii.3.
>
> 'How should he know him by whom he knows all this? How, O Beloved, should he know himself the knower?' —Bṛih., ii. 4—13.
>
> 'Unseen but seeing, unheard but hearing, unperceived but perceiving, unknown but knowing.'—Bṛih., iii. 8—11.
>
> 'Not big and not slender, not short and not long, not red and not fluid, not cloudy and not dark, not wind and not ether, not adhesive, without taste or smell, without eye or ear, without speech, without understanding, without vital force and without breath, without mouth and without size, without inner or outer.' —Bṛih., 3. 8-8.
>
> 'Invisible, incomprehensible, without pedigree, colourless, without eyes or ears, without hands or feet.' —Muṇḍ., 1. 1—6.

It is to be noted that although, according to the Upaniṣads, Brahman, the absolute reality, is unknowable, it is not unattainable, for it can be realised in immediate consciousness.

The Upaniṣads do not deal with ethical and psychological problems directly. Their enquiry is primarily of a metaphysical nature, the determination of the nature of ultimate reality, and this involves a consideration of epistemological questions as well. A study of the Upaniṣads would easily show that most of them have discovered and emphasised the great philosophic truth that the unity of consciousness is the primary factor in all experience. The fact that a strict life of self-discipline is laid down as one of the essential conditions of spiritual awakening makes it evident that, in spite of the rigorous monistic doctrine of most of the Upaniṣads and the pantheistic tendencies of some of them, moral responsibility is fully recognised.

II. THE PHILOSOPHY OF THE EPIC PERIOD.

II. THE PHILOSOPHY OF THE EPIC PERIOD.

5. General Introduction.

The Epic Period of Indian Thought covers the philosophy of the Rāmāyaṇa and the Mahābhārata including the Bhagavadgītā. The Śvetāśvatara Upaniṣad, which we have already noticed in the chapter on the Upaniṣads, and the Manusmṛiti, the Code of Manu, also belong to this period. The Rāmāyaṇa and the Mahābhārata are the two great epic poems of India, which narrate the stories of the Hindu hero Rāma and the descendants of the royal family of Bharata respectively. The Manusmṛiti is a code of religious and social law. Thus none of these works is philosophical in itself. The Bhagavadgītā, which is a part of the Mahābhārata, has however been regarded as a masterpiece of philosophical poetry, and contains abundant material which can be worked into some sort of speculative system.

The Rāmāyaṇa of Vālmīki has little philosophy in the strict sense of the term. The hero of the epic, Rāma, was a king of Ayodhyā, and in the latter part of the work he is described as the incarnation of Viṣṇu. Nothing can be said definitely about the date of this poem except that according to most of the scholars it is supposed to have been composed at a later date than the Mahābhārata, although its story belongs to an earlier period. The narration is simple and the work of one author, except the first chapter and the latter portion, which must have been added at a later date. The religion of the Rāmāyaṇa is distinctly polytheism. 'We have the Vedic gods with Indra as their chief. The new divinities of Kāma, Kubera,

Kārtikeya, Gaṅgā, Lakṣmī and Umā, the wives of Viṣṇu and Śiva, deified animals like Śeṣa the snake, Hanumat the monkey, Jāmbavat the bear, Garuḍa the eagle, Jaṭāyu the vulture, and Nandī the bull, receive prominent mention. Sacrifice is the mode of worship. Though Viṣṇu and Śiva maintain their pre-eminence, the worship of snakes, trees and rivers is also to be met with. Ideas of karma and rebirth are in the air.'*

The Manusmṛiti is primarily a code of ethics (Dharmaśāstra). By some scholars, for example, Sir William Jones, it is supposed to belong to a very early date—about 1250 B.C.; by others, for instance, Monier-Williams, it is put at about 500 B.C. The cosmology of the Manusmṛiti is the same as that of the Ṛigveda; in fact the account of creation is based upon the Hymn of Creation of the Ṛigveda which has already been quoted in a previous chapter. The religion and philosophy of Manu is chiefly the Vedic theism, although some commentators have tried to show that it contains the Sāṁkhya and the Vedānta doctrines as well. The Code dwells at length on the duties of the four castes (the *varṇas*), and the four orders of life (the *āśramas*). The four castes are: the Brāhmaṇas—priests and teachers; the Kṣatriyas—the warriors; the Vaiśyas—the traders; the Śūdras—the servant-class. The four orders of life are: the Brahmacārin—the student; the Gṛihastha—the householder; the Vānaprastha—the anchorite; the Sannyāsin—the monk.

The Mahābhārata is the most important work of this period from the philosophical point of view, for some portions of it are primarily metaphysical and ethical in nature. Besides the Bhagavadgītā, the Mokṣadharma and the Anugītā are quite interesting to a student of philosophy. The epic as a whole narrates the story of the Great War

* Rādhākriṣṇan: Indian Philosophy, vol. I, pp. 482-83.

between the two branches of the royal family of the Bhāratas—the Pāṇḍavas and the Kauravas. It is believed by scholars that the present Mahābhārata is an enlarged edition of an earlier work called the Bhārata. The epic is a complex structure made up of a number of old stories woven together and represents a mixture of the religion, civilisation and traditions of the original Aryan stock and those of the new communities with which it came into contact. In addition to the Vedic gods, Durgā, Paśupati, and Kṛiṣṇa find a prominent place and give rise to the Śākta, the Pāśupata and the Vāsudeva-Kṛiṣṇa cults respectively. The doctrines of karma and transmigration are fully recognised throughout the epic. Without going into the details of the doctrines of the other cults we shall dwell at some length on the philosophy of the Bhagavadgītā, which is based upon the doctrines of the Bhāgavata religion.

6. The Philosophy of the Bhagavadgītā.

The Bhagavadgītā or the Lord's Song is a part of the Bhīṣma Parva of the Mahābhārata. It is a dialogue between Kṛiṣṇa and Arjuna, one of the five Pāṇḍavas, on the battle-field of Kurukṣetra (near Delhi), as reported to Dhṛitarāṣṭra by Sañjaya. The occasion is the collapse of Arjuna just when he was expected to fight against the enemy. A sense of extreme despondency fills Arjuna's mind and he lays down his weapons having argued that it was no use winning a victory by killing one's own kinsmen such as the Kauravas were. The whole Gītā is a sermon from the Lord Kṛiṣṇa, who happened to be Arjuna's charioteer on the occasion, to emphasise the importance of performing one's duty even though it be unpleasant and to demonstrate the falsity of the notion that spirit is the same as the body and, therefore, liable to destruction and decay.

'Further, looking to thine own duty (*dharma*) thou shouldst not tremble: for there is nothing more welcome to a Kṣatriya than righteous war.'

'Happy the Kṣatriyas, O Pārtha, who obtain such a fight, offered unsought as an open door to heaven.'

'But if thou wilt not carry on this righteous warfare, then casting away thine own duty and thine honour, thou wilt incur sin.'—Bhag., II. 31—33.*

Speaking about the eternal and indestructible nature of the spirit and the cycle of births and deaths the Gītā says as follows :—

'Thou grievest for those that should not be grieved for, yet speakest words of wisdom (words that sound wise, but miss the deeper sense of wisdom). The wise grieveth neither for the living nor for the dead.'

'Nor at any time verily was I not, nor thou, nor the princes of men, nor verily shall we ever cease to be hereafter.'—Bhag., II. 11-12.

'Weapons cleave him not, nor fire burneth him, nor waters wet him, nor wind drieth him away.'

'Uncleavable he, incombustible he, indeed neither to be wetted nor dried away; perpetual, all-pervasive, stable, immovable, ancient.'

'Unmanifest, unthinkable, immutable he is called, therefore knowing him as such, thou shouldst not grieve.' —II. 23—25.

'Many births have been left behind by me and by thee, O Arjuna, I know them all, but thou knowest not thine, O Parantapa (one of great penance).' —IV. 5.

* English translation of these and the following verses is adopted from Annie Besant's Bhagavadgītā.

'Whenever there is decay of righteousness (*dharma*), O Bhārata, and there is exaltation of unrighteousness, then I myself come forth.'

'For the protection of the good, for the destruction of evil-doers, for the sake of firmly establishing righteousness, I am born from age to age.'—IV. 7-8.

The grand unity of the divine existence considered as the Universal Form (*viśvarūpa*) is beautifully described in the Eleventh Discourse of the Gītā :

'Behold, O Pārtha, a form of me, a hundredfold, a thousandfold, various in kind, divine, various in colours and shapes.'—XI. 5.

'Here to-day, behold the whole universe, movable and immovable, standing in one in my body, O Guḍākeśa, with aught else thou desirest to see.'—XI. 7.

Then Arjuna, having been granted divine vision, thus describes the Universal Form which he beholds :

'Within Thy form, O God, the gods I see,
All grades of beings with distinctive marks ;
Brahma, the Lord, upon His lotus-throne,
The Ṛiṣis all, and serpents, the divine.

With mouths, eyes, arms, breasts multitudinous,
I see Thee everywhere, unbounded form,
Beginning, middle, end, nor source of Thee,
Infinite Lord, infinite form, I find ;

Shining, a mass of splendour everywhere,
With discus, mace, tiara, I behold ;
Blazing as fire, as sun dazzling the gaze,
From all sides in the sky, immeasurable.

Lofty beyond all thought, unperishing,
Thou treasure-house supreme, all-immanent ;
Eternal Dharma's changeless Guardian, Thou ;
As immemorial man I think of Thee.

Nor source, nor midst, nor end ; infinite force,
Unnumbered arms, the sun and moon thine eyes,
I see thy face, as sacrificial fire
Blazing, its splendour burneth up the worlds.

By Thee alone are filled the earth, the heavens,
And all the regions that are stretched between ;
The triple worlds sink down, O mighty one,
Before Thine awful manifested form.'

—XI. 15—20

Then again:

'First of the gods, most ancient man Thou art,
Supreme receptacle of all that lives ;
Knower and known, the dwelling place on high ;
In Thy vast form the universe is spread.

Thou art Vāyu and Yama, Agni, moon,
Varuṇa, father, grandsire of all,
Hail, hail to Thee, a thousand times all hail,
Hail unto Thee, again, again all hail.

Prostrate in front of Thee, prostrate behind ;
Prostrate on every side to Thee, O All,
In power boundless, measureless in strength,
Thou holdest all : then Thou Thyself art All.'

Thus according to the Bhagavadgītā God comprehends within Himself all reality and at the same time transcends it. It is a theistic doctrine which we find in the Bhagavadgītā. Spirit and matter are both recognised as real and eternal, although the material world has been spoken of as 'Māyā,' which term is used in the Gītā simply to express that it is phenomenal and changing as distinguished from spirit which is abiding.

'Know that matter (*prakṛiti*) and spirit (*puruṣa*) are both without beginning; and know thou also that modifications and qualities (*guṇas*) are all matter-born.'

Matter is called the cause of the generation of causes and effects; spirit is called the cause of the enjoyment of pleasure and pain.

'Spirit seated in matter useth the qualities born of matter; attachment to the qualities is the cause of his birth in good and evil wombs.'

—Bhag., XII. 20—22.

The above verses distinctly embody the doctrine of spirit and matter as it was held by the earlier school of the theistic Sāṁkhya. A close study of the work clearly shows that in it a serious attempt has been made to reconcile the views of the pantheistic and the theistic as also of the monistic and the dualistic schools of thought. Similarly, in this work an effort is made to get over the antithesis between the path of action and the path of renunciation; although ultimately preference is given to 'disinterested action.'

'Renunciation of actions Thou praisest, O Kṛṣṇa, and then also Yoga (disinterested action). Of the two which is the better? That tell me conclusively,' asks Arjuna, and the Lord replies:

'Renunciation and Yoga by action both lead to the highest bliss; of the two, Yoga by action is verily better than renunciation of action.'—V. 1-2.

'Children, not sages, speak of the Sāṁkhya and the Yoga as different; he who is duly established in one obtaineth the fruits of both.'

'That place which is gained by the Sāṁkhyas is reached by the Yogis also. He seeth, who sees that the Sāṁkhya and the Yoga are one.'—V. 4 and 5.

Ritualism and the pursuit of knowledge or wisdom are similarly reconciled by giving a very wide meaning to 'sacrifice' so as to include within its scope also meditation and the pursuit of knowledge.

'Having in ancient times emanated mankind together with sacrifice, the Lord of emanation (*Prajāpati*) said: 'By this shall ye propagate; be this to you the giver of desire.'—III. 10.

'Many and various sacrifices are thus offered to the Eternal. Know thou that all these are born of action, and thus knowing thou shalt be free.'

'Better than the sacrifice of any objects is the sacrifice of wisdom, O Parantapa. All actions in their entirety, O Pārtha, culminate in wisdom.'—IV. 32-33.

'Verily there is no purifier in this world like wisdom; he that is perfected in Yoga finds it in the Self in due season.'—IV. 38.

The Yoga is described thus:—

'When a man feeleth no attachment either for the objects of sense or for actions, renouncing the formative will (*saṁkalpa*) then he is said to be enthroned in Yoga.'

The Gītā preaches a very liberal code of ethics and religion and its characteristic syncretic tendency is in evidence in this sphere also:

'However men approach me, even so do I welcome them, for the path men take from every side is Mine, O Pārtha.'—IV. 11.

In the words of Professor Rādhākṛiṣṇan, which are more or less a commentary on this same verse, 'the Gītā tries to harmonise the different ideals of life current at the time and correct their extravagances. Intellectual enquiry, strenuous self-sacrifice, fervent devotion, ceremonial observance, and yogic exercises were looked upon as offering access to the divine. The Gītā synthesises them all and shows the exact place and value of each of them.

It believes in the effectiveness of a combined attack. The harmonising ideal which all these different methods have in view is the increasing solidarity of the individual with the universe presided over by Puruṣottama.

Madhusūdana Sarasvatī considers that the Gītā adopts the three methods indicated in the Upaniṣads: *karma* or work, *upāsanā* or worship, and *jñāna* or wisdom, and devotes six chapters to each in succession. Whatever be the truth of it, it emphasises the three great divisions of conscious life. The Gītā recognises that different men are led to the same spiritual vision by different approaches, some by the perplexities of the moral life, some by the doubts of the intellect, and some by the emotional demands for perfection.

III. THE PHILOSOPHY OF THE HETERODOX SCHOOLS.

III. THE PHILOSOPHY OF THE HETERODOX SCHOOLS.

MATERIALISM.

7. The Rise of the Heterodox Systems.

No particular period can be laid down when the heterodox thought came into being. As has already been pointed out in the Introduction, all shades of thought can be traced back to the earliest ages known to us, and this is so for the simple reason that the human mind is capable of taking to any line of thought that may suggest itself in the circumstances attending the life of an individual or a community. While the majority of the Indian people have always been under the sway of one or the other of the six Hindu Schools of Philosophy, there has always been a portion of them who may be called the 'non-conformists'—those who broke away from the rest of their fellows either out of a real desire for liberty of thought or for the sake of leading a life of unfettered license.

Of the three Heterodox Systems Materialism may be taken to be as old as any other system of Indian Philosophy, and the history of Jainism too recedes almost into the pre-historic past. It is only Buddhism that begins with a definite set of doctrines—the teachings of Gautama Buddha—which can be assigned to a fixed date. We shall first take up Materialism known in Indian Philosophy as the system of the Lokāyatikas or the Cārvākas.

6

8. The System of the Lokāyatikas or the Cārvākas.

References to the followers of Materialism are found in the oldest works of Indian literature under the name of 'heretics' (*nāstikas*), and it is certain that they have always existed, although in a minority, side by side with the adherents of the orthodox creed. Materialism as a philosophy is known to be based on the authority of the aphorisms (*sūtras*) of Bṛihaspati, and the teachings of Cārvāka, after whose name it is also called the School of Cārvāka. The Materialists are also called the Lokāyatikas from the Saṁskṛit—'lokāyat,' which means 'that directed to the world of sense, or materialism.' Neither the work of Bṛihaspati nor the teachings of Cārvāka are available to us directly. It is only through the polemical works of the other Systems and the first chapter of the Sarvadarśana-saṁgraha of Mādhava that we indirectly know the doctrines of this school of thought.

The Main Doctrines of the System.—Consistently with its professed creed the system has no place for God or individual souls. Matter and the various forms of it are the only reality, and these explain all that we attribute to spiritual existence. Individual life ends with the dissolution of the body; there is no life before birth or after death. Neither is there a hell or a heaven. The authority of the sacred scriptures as the revelation of God is out of place. The only reliable criterion of truth is perception, and the only end of action is the pleasure of the senses. "Eat, drink and be merry" should be the motto of human life.

In the Vedānta-sāra of Sadānanda four different schools of Materialism are mentioned: (1) the school which considers the soul to be identical with the gross body; (2) that which identifies it with the senses; (3) that which equates it to breath and (4) that which considers it to be the same as the organ of thought. Anyhow, all of them agree in considering the soul to be a natural phenomenon.

The metaphysical and the ethical views of this system have been well summarised in a few verses quoted by the author of the Sarvadarśana-saṁgraha, and I reproduce some of them here. The following lines embody the metaphysical creed of the School:

> " In this school there are four elements, earth, water, fire and air;
> " And from these four elements alone is intelligence produced,
> " Just like the intoxicating power from 'kiṇva,'* etc., mixed together.
> " Since in 'I am fat,' 'I am lean,' these attributes abide in the same subject,
> " And since fatness, etc., reside only in the body, it alone is the soul and no other,
> " And such phrases as 'my body' are only significant metaphorically."

The ethical teachings of the school are given in the following verses:

> " While life is yours, live joyously;
> None can escape Death's searching eye;
> When once this frame of ours they burn,
> How shall it e'er again return ? "

And again in the following:

> "The pleasure which arises to men from contact with sensible objects,

* A drug or seed used to cause fermentation in the manufacture of spirits.

Is to be relinquished as accompanied by pain—such
is the reasoning of fools;
The berries of paddy, rich with the finest white grains,
What man, seeking his true interest, would fling
away because covered with husk and dust?"

The following lines which have been attributed to Bṛihaspati, will be found interesting as a remarkable, although slightly exaggerated expression of the tenets of this school :—

"The fire is hot, the water cold, refreshing cool the breeze of morn;
By whom came this variety? from their own nature was it born."

and again—

"There is no heaven, no final liberation, nor any soul in another world,
Nor do the actions of the four castes, orders, etc., produce any real effect.
The Agnihotra, the three Vedas, the ascetic's three staves, and smearing one's self with ashes,
Were made by Nature, as the livelihood of those destitute of knowledge and manliness.
If a beast slain in the Jyotiṣṭoma rite will itself go to heaven,
Why then does not the sacrificer forthwith offer his own father?
If the Śrāddha produces gratification to beings who are dead,
Then here, too, in the case of travellers when they start, it is needless to give provisions for the journey.
If beings in heaven are gratified by our offering the Śrāddha here,
Then why not give the food down below to those who are standing on the house-top?
While life remains let a man live happily, let him feed on 'ghee' even though he runs in debt;

When once the body becomes ashes, how can it ever return again ?
If he who departs from the body goes to another world,
How is it that he comes not back again, restless for love of his kindred ?
Hence it is only as a means of livelihood that Brāhmaṇas have established here
All these ceremonies for the dead,—there is no other fruit anywhere."

JAINISM.

9. General Introduction to the System.

As I have indicated already, the origin of Jainism seems to recede into the prehistoric past, and it is quite certain that it is much older than Buddhism. According to the orthodox belief the Jaina religion is eternal, and it has been revealed to mankind through a succession of divine teachers called the Tīrthaṅkaras. During the present cycle, Ṛiṣabha was the first Tīrthaṅkara and Vardhamān Mahāvīra the last (twenty-fourth). Pārśva was the predecessor of Mahāvīra, and is believed to have lived 250 years before him. Mahāvīra, being the latest and the most important teacher, is usually taken as the founder of Jainism in its present form.

Vardhamān was a Kṣatriya prince, and was born at Vaisāli, the modern Besarh, 27 miles to the north of Patnā. According to the tradition, he was born in 599 B.C. and died in 527 B.C., and thus he was the senior contemporary of the great Buddha. At the age of twenty-eight he, like Buddha, is reported to have renounced his home and taken to a spiritual career of penance and religious teaching. After a period of twelve years of preparatory life characterised by austerities and self-mortification he attained 'enlightenment,' and consequently became a prophet—a Tīrthaṅkara—and received the titles of Jina (the spiritual conqueror) and Mahāvīra (the great hero). He taught for thirty years after his enlightenment, and during this period he organised his order of monks. He received considerable support in his mission from the Kṣatriya ruling princes of his time—he being one of them in the early part of his life.

On the ground of the similarity of the doctrines and the lives of the two teachers and also because they were contemporaries, one or two European writers, for example, Barth, quoted by Prof. Rādhākṛṣṇan, tend to think that Mahāvīra and Buddha are not two different personalities and that Jainism arose, in the course of time, as a mere offshoot of Buddhism. However, the researches of Colebrooke, Jacobi and Bühler have already established beyond doubt that the two names represent two independent personalities, and that Jainism is an independent religion and one much older than the oldest form of Buddhism.

There are two chief sects of Jainism: (1) the Śvetāmbaras (wearers of white cloth) and the Digambaras (the naked). These agree with each other so far as their main creed is concerned, but differ on certain points of detail. For instance, the Digambaras believe that the Tīrthaṅkaras lived without food; that a monk who owns property and wears clothes cannot achieve salvation; and that women cannot obtain 'mokṣa.' They do not accept the canonical works of the other sect, and claim to have preserved the original teachings and practices of the Jaina religion. There are reasons to believe that the Digambaras represent the older creed.

10. Outlines of Jaina Philosophy.

It has already been pointed out that Jainism, although a religious doctrine, represents one of the heterodox schools of Indian Thought. It does not believe in the authority of the Vedas and the other sacred scriptures of the Hindus. It has also been called an atheistic philosophy for the reason that it does not recognise the agency and control of God in the creation and preservation of the universe. Jainism has its own prophets—the Tīrthaṅkaras as they are called, and its own scriptures, which are the teachings of these semi-divine beings. It is on the basis of these works that the religion and philosophy of the Jainas are founded.

Jaina Metaphysics.—To begin with, there are two exhaustive categories, *viz.*, that of the 'living' or 'souls' (*jīva*) and that of the 'non-living' (*ajīva*). The one is entirely distinct from the other. Souls (*jīvas*) are infinite in number, and are possessed of infinite perception (*ananta-darśana*), infinite knowledge (*ananta-jñāna*), infinite bliss (*ananta-sukha*) and infinite power (*ananta-vīrya*). These perfections are however suppressed by the presence of the body which is determined by one's actions (*karman*). Souls are substances (*dravya*) and are eternal. They have no particular fixed size and adjust themselves to the size of the body which they have to invest because of their 'karma.' They fill the whole body just as light or air would fill a room. The smallest conceivable particle of matter is also invested with a soul, or rather, with a cluster of souls, and thus the whole world is saturated with these living entities called the 'nigodas.' These 'nigodas' bear a remarkable resemblance to the 'monads' in the philosophy of Leibnitz. Thus Jainism stands for a kind of animistic theory of the universe.

Souls are divided into two classes, *viz.*, the mundane and the released. The former are in a state of bondage and are subject to transmigration from one form of mundane life to another. The latter are those who have destroyed the conditions of their bondage and are, therefore, liberated from the cycle of births and deaths. Then there is a further subdivision of the mundane souls according to the degree of their intelligence, the number of their sense-organs and their power of locomotion in the physical bodies which they possess.

A very elaborate theory of 'Karman' is worked out in the Jaina philosophy in order to explain the character and the fate of individual souls in their mundane existence. It is actions which obscure the perfect nature of the soul and bind it to earthly life as they go on accumulating. Consequently, the right means of self-realisation and emancipation is to be found in the purging away of these actions and their effects. This process is known as 'nirjara' as distinguished from the opposite one of 'āsrava,' which represents the influx of the 'karma-matter' into the soul. Each of these two processes is of two kinds: (1) those mental activities of the soul through which and on account of which, the 'karma-matter' enters the soul are called 'bhāvāsrava,' while (2) the actual entrance of this matter into the soul is known as 'karmāsrava.' Similarly, (1) the mental effort by means of which the 'karma-matter' is destroyed is called 'bhāva-nirjara,' and (2) the actual destruction of this matter is known as the 'dravyanirjara.' These processes are further subdivided into a number of distinctions which are too numerous to be noticed in a brief treatise like this. A complete destruction of all the 'karmans' leads to liberation (*mokṣa*).

The second category of 'non-living' (*ajīva*) has been divided rather loosely into (*i*) matter (*pudgalāstikya*), (*ii*) the principle of motion or activity (*dharmāstikya*), (*iii*) the principle of rest or inactivity (*adharmāstikya*), (*iv*) ether (*ākāśāstikya*), (*v*) time (*kāla*), (*vi*) righteousness (*puṇya*), and (*vii*) sin (*pāpa*). These are explained as follows :

(*i*) *Matter* (*pudgalāstikya*) is made up of atoms (*aṇu*) which are without size and eternal. It is either gross—such as that of which visible things are made, or subtle—such as that which forms the stuff of the 'karma particles,' and is invisible. All things are made of atoms, and their character is determined by the geometrical modes and the arrangements of the constituent atoms. Things change because of a change in the modes of their atoms.

(*ii*) *The Principle of Motion or Activity* (*dharmāstikya*).—The terms 'dharma' and 'adharma' have a peculiar significance in Jainism. 'Dharma' is the principle or condition of motion or activity—that which makes all motion possible—although in itself it is not motion. It pervades the whole mundane universe, and hence renders action possible. Hence the mundane universe is the world of action, and consequently of bondage.

(*iii*) *The Principle of Rest or Inactivity* (*adharmāstikya*).—On the other hand, the term 'adharma' signifies the principle or condition of rest or inactivity—that which renders motion or activity impossible. It pervades the universe of the liberated souls and hence helps them there to keep themselves at rest and enjoy peace in spite of their inherent activity.

(*iv*) ***Ether*** (*ākāśāstikya*) is another pervasive entity, which makes it possible for both the living and the non-living to exist in this and the other world. It is not a negation of obstruction, but a positive entity.

(*v*) ***Time*** (*kāla*) is the principle or condition of change in atoms and things made of these. It does not produce change by itself, but no change can take place without it. It admits of such modifications of itself as moments, hours, days, etc., and is a substance (*dravya*).

(*vi*) ***Righteousness*** (*puṇya*) is the cause of pleasure or happiness.

(*vii*) ***Sin*** (*pāpa*) is the cause of pain or misery.

According to Jainism the world is eternal—without a beginning or an end. It consists of three parts—(*i*) the High Regions (*ūrdhvaloka*), where the gods reside; (*ii*) the Middle Regions (*madhyaloka*)—the world of human beings; and (*iii*) the Nether World (*adholoka*), where the denizens of hell reside. It is to the High Regions characterised by inactivity or peace, that the souls repair after they are liberated from the world of bondage.

The Theory of Knowledge in Jainism.—To begin with, knowledge is of two kinds:—(*i*) perceptual and (*ii*) non-perceptual, known as *pratyakṣa* and *parokṣa* respectively.

(i) *Perceptual knowledge* (*pratyakṣa*) is the direct cognition of objects. It reveals them as they are. In perceptual knowledge there are both subjective and objective elements. The subjective aspect of it is determined by the nature of the individual percipient, while the objective side depends upon certain external conditions affecting the presentation of the perceived objects, such as the presence of light for visual perception, and the fitness of the sense-organs, etc. According to the Jainas, there is no indeterminate (*nirvikalpa*) stage in perceptual knowledge. It is determinate (*savikalpa*) from the very outset. It may be of four kinds : (*a*) That derived through the senses (*upalabdhi*); (*b*) That derived through clairvoyance of objects removed in space and time (*avadhi*) ; (*c*) A direct knowledge of the ideas of others such as is obtained in telepathy—(*manaḥ-paryāya*) and (*d*) Perfect knowledge of all reality in its various forms, as it is to an omniscient mind, unlimited by time and space (*kevala*). Such knowledge is possessed by the liberated souls only.

(ii) *Non-perceptual knowledge* (*parokṣa*) does not give as vivid a representation of objects as perceptual knowledge does. It includes inference, imagination, memory, etc. According to the Jainas, it is not necessary to employ five propositions in a syllogism, as is done in the Nyāya Logic. They think that the first two steps are quite sufficient to enable us to draw an inference. Thus a syllogism in Jaina Logic is as follows:—

1. The hill is fiery,
2. Because of smoke.

However, it is recognised that in order to convince such an ignorant being as a child it may be necessary to employ all the five steps of reasoning formulated in the Nyāya Logic.

As for proof by Testimony, as has already been pointed out, the Jainas do not recognise the authority of the Vedas. It is only the Jaina scriptures that can give right knowledge.

It may be mentioned that Jaina Psychology recognises the important fact that the subject, the object and the act of knowledge itself are all inseparable and interdependent factors in the concrete unity of cognition.

The Doctrine of Relativity in Jainism—the Theory of the Relativity of Being (the Saptabhaṅgīnaya) and the Relativity of Predication (the Syādvāda).—According to the Jaina theory of Being, every form of reality can be looked at from different points of view. These are called the *nayas*, which are classified under seven heads, and the whole doctrine is known as the *Saptabhaṅgīnaya*. Further, a statement, which is true about a thing from one of these points of view, may be false, judged from a different point of view, and *vice versa*. Hence no statement is absolutely true or false, and all that we can say is that something 'may be so' or 'it may not be so.' This doctrine of the relativity of predication has been called the *Syādvāda*.

The alternative ways of considering the being of things are as follows:

(1) When we consider the various qualities of a thing as unified in, and identical with, the

thing itself, this point of view is called the *dravyanaya.*

(2) When we think of the qualities separately from the thing to which they are supposed to belong, and hold that it is only the qualities which represent reality, and that there is no substance beyond them, this view is called the *paryāyanaya.*

These two *nayas* are further subdivided into seven forms, the *dravyanaya* into three, and the *paryāyanaya* into four.

The three forms of the first are as follows :—

(*i*) The *Naigamanaya*—the common-sense point of view, or the superficial way of looking at things ; for example, a book may be considered as a mere collection of sheets of paper.

(*ii*) The *Saṁgrahanaya*—according to which a thing is looked at from the most general point of view—as simply ' being. '

(*iii*) The *Vyavahāranaya* is that which considers a thing from the empirical or the practical point of view, as it is revealed to us in experience in its general and particular form of being, that is to say, as something permanent as well as changing, and as serviceable to us in a number of ways.

The four forms of the *paryāyanaya* are as follows :—

(*vi*) The *Ṛijusūtranaya*—which considers a thing as it presents itself at any particular moment. According to this view everything is in a state of continual transition and there is no continuity or identity.

(*v*) The *Śabdanaya*—that which holds that the relation between terms and their meaning is relative. A term refers to a certain object because it has been made to stand for it, and several terms may refer to one and the same object.

(*vi*) The *Samābhirūḍhanaya* is that which distinguishes between words according to the meaning of the roots from which they are derived.

(*vii*) *The Evambhūtanaya* is a special form of the sixth *naya* and holds that etymologically a term refers to an object looked at only in one particular aspect of its existence, and that, therefore, it is only with reference to that particular aspect of the thing that the term should be used.

According to the Jainas, the Nyāya and the Vaiśeṣika systems look at things from the first point of view, the monistic Vedānta from the second standpoint; the Sāṁkhya from the third, and the Buddhists from the fourth point of view. And as these take these respective standpoints as representing the whole truth about a thing, they are guilty of what is called in Jaina Philosophy the Naya-fallacy (*nayābhāsa*).

Closely allied to and dependent upon the doctrine of the Relativity of Being—the *Saptabhaṅgīnaya*,—is the Theory of the Relativity of Predication—the *Syādvāda*. According to it there are seven ways of speaking about a thing and its attributes. These are explained as follows :—

(*i*) *May be, it is* (*syād asti*)—this is used when we refer to a thing from the point of view of its own material, size, shape, time and place. For example, reference may be made to a particular jar, made of clay, of particular dimensions and shape, lying in one's room at a particular time.

(*ii*) *May be, it is not* (*syād nāsti*)—employed when we consider a thing from the point of view of a different material, shape, size, time and place. For instance, a particular jar of clay is not as made of iron, and as one of a different shape and size, and as existing at a different time and place.

(*iii*) *May be, it is and it is not* (*syād asti nāsti*)—when we look at a thing from the first and the second standpoints at one and the same time.

(*iv*) *May be, it is not predicable* (*syād avaktavya*)—when we want to express the impossibility of predicating of one and the same thing two contradictory statements according to the first and the second standpoints.

(*v*) *May be, it is and yet not predicable* (*syād asti avaktavya*)—when we note the existence of a thing from the point of view of its own nature, and at the same time, also the unpredicability of two contradictory statements from the fourth point of view.

(*vi*) *May be, it is not and not predicable* (*syād nāsti avaktavya*)—when we combine the second and the fourth standpoints together, that is to say, when we note the non-existence of a thing from a certain point of view, and also the unpredicability of two contradictory statements about it.

(*vii*) *May be, it is and it is not, and not predicable* (*syād asti nāsti avaktavya*)—when we combine the first, the second and the fourth standpoints, that is to say, when we note the existence and non-existence of a thing and also the indescribability of the same by means of two contradictory statements.

One can easily see that it is only the first and the second standpoints that are fundamentally important and characteristic of the usual modes of our thinking and predication. The rest are simply a formal elaboration of these two ways of speaking about the things of our experience.

Bondage and Emancipation in Jainism.—'Bondage is the condition of being unseparated, with a mutual interpenetration of parts between the soul and the body.' The causes of bondage are—(*i*) False Intuition; (*ii*) Non-indifference; (*iii*) Carelessness and (*iv*) Sin.

(*i*) *False Intuition* is want of faith in the teachings of the Jaina prophets. It is of two kinds: (*a*) *Innate*—that due to one's own character, which is determined by the influence of one's former actions; and (*b*) *Derived*—that due to the influence of others.

(*ii*) *Non-indifference* is the want of restraint of the five senses and the internal organ from the objects of experience.

(*iii*) *Caerlessness* is the want of effort to practise penance.

(*iv*) *Sin* consists of anger and other similar passions.

There are subdivisions of bondage which are not mentioned here for fear of prolixity.

Emancipation (*mokṣa*) is the absolute release from all actions by the decay (*nirjara*) of the causes of bondage and of existence.

(*i*) Right Intuition, (*ii*) Right Knowledge and (*iii*) Right Conduct are the means of liberation. These are explained as follows :

(*i*) ***Right Intuition*** (*Śraddhā*) is absolute faith in the teachings of a Jaina prophet—a Jina. It is either natural to a man or due to the instruction of a teacher.

(*ii*) ***Right Knowledge*** (*Jñāna*) is a knowledge of the predicaments, soul, etc., as they really are, unvitiated by the defects of illusion or doubt. It is of several kinds, as explained already.

(*iii*) ***Right Conduct*** (*Carita*) is the entire renunciation of all evil impulses and the practising of the five vows of (*a*) Absolute harmlessness (*ahiṁsā*), (*b*) Truthfulness (*sūnṛitā*), (*c*) Honesty or non-stealing (*asteya*), (*d*) Chastity (*brahmacarya*) and (*e*) Disinterestedness (*aparigraha*). It may be mentioned that these five principles are the same as the five 'yamas' of the Yoga philosophy.

Elaborate details of what may be called the Jaina system of Yoga are further given, and all of them fall under one or the other of the above three main heads.

The Jaina Doctrines Summarised.—The following summary of the Jaina doctrines as given by Jinadatta is reproduced from Cowell's English translation of the Sarvadarśana-saṁgraha : "The hindrances belonging to vigour, enjoyment, sensual pleasure, giving and receiving, sleep, fear, ignorance, aversion, laughter, liking, disliking, love, hatred, want of indifference, desire, sorrow, deceit, these are the eighteen 'faults' (*doṣa*) according to our system. The divine Jina is our Guru, who declares the true knowledge of the *tattvas.* The path of emancipation consists of knowledge, intuition and conduct.

There are two means of proof (*pramāṇa*) in the *Syādvāda* doctrine—sense-perception and inference.

All consists of the eternal and the non-eternal; there are nine or seven *tattvas.* The *jīva*, the *ajīva*, merit and demerit, *āsrava*, *saṁvara*, *bandha*, *nirjara*, *mukti*—we shall now explain each. *Jīva* is defined as intelligence; *ajīva* is all other than it; merit means bodies which arise from good actions, demerit the opposite; *āsrava* is the bondage of actions, *nirjara* is the unloosing thereof; *mokṣa* arises from the destruction of the eight forms of *karman* or action. But by some teachers 'merit' is included in *saṁvara*, and demerit in *āsrava*."

"A woman attains not the highest knowledge, she enters not Mukti,—so say the Digambaras; but there is a great division on this point between them and the Śvetāmbaras."

11. Jaina Literature.

The earliest literature of the Jainas consists of the fourteen Pūrvas and the eleven Aṅgas. The Pūrvas have been lost altogether, and the Aṅgas have come down to us, although, according to the Digambaras, these too do not represent the original texts. An extensive literature comprising of glosses and commentaries has sprung up round these works. Some of the later important works are Umāsvāti's Tattvārthābhigamasūtra (1—85 A.D.), Tarkavārtika, Nemicandra's Dravyasaṁgraha, Mallisena's Syādvādamañjarī, Siddhasena Divākara's Nyāyāvatāra, Anantavīrya's Parīkṣāmukhasūtralaghuvṛitti, Prabhācandra's Prameyakamalamārtaṇḍa, Hemacandra's Yogaśāstra, and Devasūri's Pramāṇanayatattvālokālaṅkāra. All these, except the first, were written between the sixth and the twelfth century A.D.

It may be mentioned here that, besides works on religion and philosophy, the Jainas have also made valuable contributions to grammar, poetics and other branches of knowledge.

BUDDHISM.

12. Gautama Buddha and his Philosophy.

Gautama Buddha, the founder of Buddhism, was born about 560 B.C., near Kapilavastu, in the Lumbino Grove. His father, Śuddhodana, was a Kṣatriya prince of the Śākya clan, and his mother was the daughter of a neighbouring Kṣatriya chief. It is said that it was foretold that Gautama would renounce the world when he should see a decrepit old man, a diseased man, a dead man and an ascetic. The father, being naturally anxious to prevent his son from taking to the life of a recluse, married him early and surrounded him with all kinds of luxuries. However, as fate would have it, on successive occasions, when Gautama went out of his palace, he did meet the objects, the sight of which was to be the occasion of his renunciation, and he left the royal abode when he was twenty-nine years old, leaving at home a devoted wife and a newly-born son. For about six years, after this event, he practised hard penance in order to attain Truth, but he ultimately found that self-mortification was not the right way to achieve his aim, and consequently, he gave up that kind of life and took to an ordinary course of contemplation. Shortly after he did attain the supreme enlightenment, and thus became

Buddha (the enlightened). For full forty years after this attainment of Truth he travelled widely throughout India and preached his doctrine. He passed away when he was over eighty years of age leaving behind him a devoted band of disciples who carried on the work of preaching his gospel in India and outside. It is almost too well-known to need mention here that Buddhism has been one of the most successful missionary religions that the world has ever witnessed.

The Essentials of Buddhism.—As the result of his enlightenment Gautama lay down two formulas as the fundamental principles of his teaching. These are : (1) The Four Noble Truths (*āryasatyāni*) and (2) The Twelvefold Concatenation of Causes and Effects (*pratītyasamutpāda*). They are explained as follows :—

The Four Noble Truths (*āryasatyāni*) declare the existence of (*i*) Suffering (*dukkha*) ; (*ii*) the cause of suffering (*samudaya*) ; (*iii*) the possibility of the suppression of suffering (*nirodha*) and (*iv*) the way or means of the suppression of suffering (*pratipad* or *mārga*).

These four truths correspond exactly to the four cardinal articles of Āyurveda—the Medical Science of India, *viz.*, the existence of disease ; the cause of disease ; the possibility of the suppression of disease and the treatment of disease. They have been applied to the spiritual healing of mankind, Buddha himself being, in fact, called a doctor in the Lalitavistāra.

The Twelvefold Concatenation of Causes and Effects, called the *Pratītyasamutpāda* or the *Nidānas* (causes), is an analysis of the fundamental cause of evil. The following are the various factors constituting the series: (*i*) Ignorance (*avidyā*); (*ii*) Impressions (*saṁskāras*); (*iii*) Clear Consciousness (*vijñāna*) ; (*iv*) Name and Form (*nāmarūpa*); (*v*) the six organs of sense (*ṣaḍāyatana*); (*vi*) Contact of the senses with exterior objects (*sparśa*); (*vii*) Feeling (*vedanā*); (*viii*) Desire (*tṛiṣṇā*); (*ix*) Attachment (*upādāna*); (*x*) Becoming or the beginning of existence (*bhava*); (*xi*) Birth or actual existence (*jāti*); (*xii*) Misery of old age and death and other forms of suffering attending worldly existence.

It will appear from this list that like the other systems of Indian Philosophy, in Buddhism too, 'ignorance' (*avidyā*) is laid down as the root cause of all evil and suffering. The series has been interpreted in a number of ways so as to take it to represent the diagram of human life and to explain the psychological and physical development of an individual organic being. One of these explanations of this chain of causes and effects is given here by way of illustration :—

Before the appearance of life there is want of consciousness or ignorance (*avidyā*) ... (i)

With the appearance of life there is half-consciousness or vague impressions (*saṃskāras*) ... (ii)

Then follows the state of clear consciousness or knowledge (*vijñāna*) ... ... (iii)

Next appears Experience which involves :—

The presentation of objects under 'name and form' (*nāmarūpa*) ... ... (iv)

The activity of the six organs of sense (*ṣaḍāyatana*) ... ... (v)

The contact of the organs with the presented objects (*sparśa*) ... ... (vi)

Perception is followed by some kind of feeling (*vedanā*) ... ... (vii)

Feeling arouses desire (*tṛiṣṇā*) ... ... (viii)

Desire is the cause of attachment to the objects of desire (*upādāna*) ... ... (ix)

Attachment introduces the beginning of the realisation of the object of desire (*bhava*) ... (x)

Effort to realise the object of desire leads to the actual realisation of it (*jāti*) ... ... (xi)

The realised object must come to an end, or meet destruction, and hence, produce pain and a number of miseries ... ... (xii)

The correspondence of some of the factors in the above series to those of the Sāṁkhya theory of creation is worth notice :—

Ignorance (*avidyā*) corresponds to Primordial Matter (*pradhāna*).

Impressions (*saṁkāras*) correspond to Intellect (*buddhi*).

Clear Consciousness (*vijñāna*) corresponds to Egoism (*ahaṁkāra*).

Name and Form (*nāmarūpa*) correspond to the Six Subtle Elements (*tanmātrāṇi*).

Six Sense-organs (*ṣaḍāyatana*) correspond to sense-organs (*indriyāṇi*).

That the above list of the 'nidānas' has been formulated with reference to the development of the psychical and the physical life of organic beings is plain from the explanation of the fourth of them, *viz.*, 'Name and Form.'

'Name' (*nāman*) denotes all mental or internal phenomena, and 'Form' (*rūpa*) signifies all physical or external phenomena. 'Name' includes generally four of the five 'elements of existence' (*skandhas*)—*viz.*, Feeling (*vedanā*); Notion (*saṁjñā*); Mental dispositions (*saṁskāras*) and Clear Consciousness (*vijñāna*). 'Form' comprehends the four physical elements (*mahābhūtāni*) —*viz.*, earth, water, fire, air and their composite forms. Thus it would appear that 'name and form' (*nāmarūpa*) and the 'elements of existence' (*skandhas*) are co-extensive terms. There are further fifty-two subdivisions of 'mental dispositions' (*saṁskāras*) and eighty-nine subdivisions of 'clear consciousness' (*vijñāna*). These are too numerous to explain here and do not possess any very great philosophical importance.

The aggregate of 'names and forms' (*skandhas*) goes to form what we should call an individual being, and what is known as 'pudgala' in Buddhism, although there is nothing like individuality in this system of philosophy. There is no individual soul apart from these elements of existence.

The cause of the aggregation of these 'skandhas,' that is to say, of birth, is action (*karman*) which is supposed to have no beginning, but which can have an end. So long as the course of action lasts, there is a repetition of birth and death, which mean nothing more than an integration and disintegration of the elements of existence.

The way to stop the working of 'karman' is to follow the eightfold path preached by Buddha in his First Discourse. It consists of : (1) Right Belief ; (2) Right Feeling ; (3) Right Speech ; (4) Right Action ; (5) Right Livelihood ; (6) Right Endeavour ; (7) Right Memory and (8) Right Meditation.

There are four stages on the way to the Final Deliverance or 'Disappearance,' and four distinct names have been given to those who are in each of these stages : *viz.*, *Srotāpanna*, *Sakṛidgāmin*, *Anāgāmin*, and *Arhat*. The common designation of all the disciples of Buddha is *Śrāvaka* or *Sāvaka*.

Deliverance, known as *nirvāṇa* in Buddhism, is of two kinds, or rather of two degrees : (i) The First or the Secondary 'Nirvāṇa' which is attainable by the *Arhats* even in the present life, and is something like the *jīvanmukti* of Hinduism; (ii) The Final or the Absolute 'Nirvāṇa,' which can be attained only after death, and is known as the *Parinirvāṇa* in the case of a Buddha.

It is somewhat difficult to give an exact definition of 'nirvāṇa,' and Buddha himself was not quite clear on this point. Rhys Davids defines it as "the extinction of that sinful, grasping condition of mind and heart, which would otherwise, according to the great mystery of 'karma,' be the cause of renewed individual existence," and this description of it seems to be well nigh correct.

Besides these doctrines, there is, in Buddhism, a very complex and exhaustive classification of the various regions into which the universe can be divided and of the beings that inhabit them.

There is also a very elaborate scheme of the spiritual exercises enjoined for those who seek deliverance. In essence these are for the most part the same as the Yoga practices of the other Indian systems.

13. The Four Main Schools of Buddhism.

With the spread of Buddhism in India and outside there sprung up a number of schools of Buddhistic Thought, some of which held very divergent views about the nature of the world. In fact, every country, which received the gospel of Buddha, developed its own Church in the course of time, and it should be the function of an ecclesiastical history of Buddhism to give an account of the origin and growth of these churches. For a philosophical review of Buddhism it should be sufficient to notice the four main schools of Buddhistic Thought, which flourished in India about the time when Fa-Hian, the Chinese traveller, visited the country. Two of these—those of the *Vaibhāṣikas* and the *Sautrāntikas*—

professed a form of Realism and were attached to the *Hīnayāna* section of Buddhism; while the other two, *viz.*, those of the *Yogācāras* or the *Vijñānavādins* and the *Mādhyamikas* represented Idealism and belonged to the *Mahāyāna* Creed.

The Hīnayāna Doctrine.—The *Hīnayāna*, which literally means the 'smaller path,' was the name given to the earlier form of Buddhism, the teachings of which were nearer to those of Buddha, and it was so called by the later school of Mahāyānism either because, according to it, the earlier school represented an inferior doctrine, or because it suggested a shorter path to deliverance. The general characteristics of Hīnayānism are the following :—

(*i*) The soul or ego is only a complex of incongruous transitory elements (*skandhas*), which endures by means of desire (or thirst) alone.

(*ii*) Salvation can be attained even after present life by the killing of all desire and contemplating the Four Noble Truths (*āryasatyāni*).

(*iii*) The ideal moral life is that of a Buddhist monk.

(*iv*) Buddhism is not necessarily a cult of devotion to Buddha, who is neither a god nor a supernatural being.

(*v*) Buddhism is not merely a vehicle of deliverance, but also teaches one how to be reborn in heaven.

There are two schools in *Hīnayānism* :

1. *The School of the Vaibhāṣikas*—the doctrines of which are based upon the *Abhidharma*—an early Buddhist writing. It holds that the phenomenal world is real and that we have a direct perception of exterior objects.

According to it, Buddha was a common human being who obtained 'Nirvāṇa' by virtue of his enlightenment—'Buddhahood'—and finally passed away into nothingness.

2. *The School of the Sautrāntikas*—which recognised the authority of the Sūtras only. It also represents a realistic doctrine, but holds that the perception of exterior objects is not direct but takes place only through their images. The question, whether the objects perceived have any form of their own, or whether their form is simply imposed upon them by the mind, is a disputed one with this system.

The Mahāyāna Doctrine.—Mahāyānism or the Great Vehicle represents a later phase of Buddhism, and is either an extreme form of idealism or nihilism. Its philosophy may be briefly analysed as follows :

(*i*) In contrast to Hīnayānism it holds that the path of deliverance is not a short one, for it requires a succession of lives to attain the complete 'Nirvāṇa.' For the same reason it is called the doctrine of the Great Vehicle or Path.

(*ii*) The ancient doctrine about the nature of the soul is incomplete, for the elements of existence (*skandhas*) themselves, which are supposed to constitute it, are void, that is to say, they do not exist.

(*iii*) The way to 'Nirvāṇa' consists in the acquiring of the wisdom or knowledge that all is vacuity or void, and in practising devotion to Buddha or the Bodhisattvas (the future Buddhas) who are either gods already, or become gods, in the course of time. The ideal life is that which aims at practising the virtues (*pāramitās*) of a future Buddha (a Bodhisattva), as they are explained in the scriptures.

Mahāyānism emphasises the path of devotion (*bhakti-mārga*) and under its influence there developed in Buddhism a distinct sect in imitation of the *Bhaktimārga* of Hinduism.

The two philosophical schools of Mahāyānism are the following :—

1. *The School of the Vijñānavādins or the Yogācāras*, which holds that nothing is real except consciousness or the states of consciousness (*vijñāna*). It is thus a form of Idealism. Aśvaghoṣa was one of the prominent exponents of this school.

2. *The School of the Mādhyamikas.*—The Mādhyamikas are complete nihilists. Like the Vedāntists they teach that the whole phenomenal world is a mere illusion, and like them they also recognise two kinds of truth—the real or ultimate (*pāramārthika*), and the unreal or illusory (*saṁvṛiti*). In fact the second kind of truth is no truth at all, and hence "there is no existence, there is no cessation of being; there is no birth, there is no 'nirvāṇa'; there is no difference between those who have attained 'nirvāṇa' and those who have not. All conditions, in fact, are like dreams."

Buddhistic Ethics.—In the sphere of morals Buddhism usually adopted most of the injunctions of the prevalent moral code and showed considerable regard for the conventional morality of the Hindus. Morals had a place even in a system of Buddhistic Nihilism, for, as Kern says, according to it, "the force of illusion is irresistible, and as all distinctions are equally an illusion, the distinction of good and evil, of virtue and vice, remains unaffected. The reasonable objection that if all is illusion, their idea of illusion is as non-existent as all the rest, would fail to trouble those philosophers, because in their system, the decrees of Reason are not only fallible, but absolutely false."

Buddhism and the other Systems.—In its atheism Buddhism is akin to Jainism and the Sāṁkhya system. Its Idealism and Nihilism show traces of resemblance to the monistic tendencies of the Vedānta. That Buddhism has been influenced by all the contemporary schools of thought, in some way or the other, is a fact beyond doubt. We have already seen that Vardhamāna Mahāvīra, the reputed teacher of Jainism, was the senior contemporary of Buddha, and the similarity between Buddhism and Jainism, especially, in the sphere of morals and disciplinary exercises, is only too evident. In spite of the great divergence of its doctrines, Brāhmaṇism was not without its influence upon Buddhism. We see this clearly in the code of Buddhistic morals, and in the Buddhistic doctrine of the transmigration of the *Skandhas*, in spite of the fact that the existence of souls is definitely denied. The theory of 'karma' also points to the same source.

14. A Summary of Buddhistic Doctrines.

The following description of the Buddhistic doctrines is reproduced from the Viveka-vilāsa as it has been quoted in the Sarvadarśana-saṁgraha (Gough's English Translation).

> "Of the Bauddhas Sugata (Buddha) is the deity and the Universe is momentarily fluxional;

The following four principles in order are to be known by the name of the noble truths :—

Pain, the inner seats, and from them an aggregate is held,
And the path (method) ; of all this let the explication be heard in order.
Pain, and the *skandhas* of the embodied one, which are declared to be five,—
Sensation, consciousness, name, impression and form.
The five organs of sense, the five objects of sense, sound and the rest, the common sensory,
And (the intellect) the abode of merit,—these are the twelve inner seats.
This should be the complement of desire and so forth, when it arises in the heart of man.
Under the name of soul's own nature, it should be the aggregate.
The fixed idea that all impressions are momentary,
This is to be known as the path, and is also styled as emancipation.
Furthermore, there are two instruments of science, perception and inference.
The Bauddhas are well-known to be divided into four sects, the Vaibhāṣikas and the rest.
The Vaibhāṣika highly esteens an object concomitant to the cognition ;
The Sautrāntika allows no external object apprehensible by perception ;
The Yogācāra admits only intellect accompanied with forms ;
The Mādhyamikas hold mere consciousness self-subsistent.
All the four (sects of) Bauddhas proclaim the same emancipation,
Arising from the extirpation of desire, etc., the stream of cognitions and impressions.
The skin garment, the water-pot, the tonsure, the rags, the single meal in the forenoon,
The congregation and the red vesture are adopted by the Bauddha mendicants."

15. Sacred Books of Buddhism.

The earliest sacred literature of Buddhism consists of the Tripiṭaka—the three-fold basket of Law, comprising the Vinayapiṭaka, the Suttapiṭaka and the Abhidhammapiṭaka. The Vinaya treats chiefly of the disciplinary rules of monks. The Suttapiṭaka is much more extensive and diversified, and treats in a loose way of the various subjects relating to doctrine. It is divided into five Nikāyas peculiar to the Theravāda or the older creed of Buddhism. The greater bulk of the Piṭaka can be assigned to about the 3rd Century B.C. The Abhidhamma deals with the same subjects as the Suttapiṭaka, but it does so in a more scholastic and technical manner. It is full of definitions and classifications of the various subjects of importance, and was probably developed during the period between the Councils of Vesālī and Pāṭaliputra.

The Mahāvastu is another important work which belongs to the school of the Lokottaravādins—a subdivision of the Mahāsāṅghikas. It contains the legendary life of the Bodhisattva—the Jātakas without any admixture of matters of discipline. It is probably posterior to the reign of Aśoka.

According to Huein Thsang, the old Mahāsāṅghika canon was five-fold :—Sūtra; Vinaya ; Abhidhamma ; Saṁyukta and Dhāraṇi- (or Vidyādhara-) Piṭaka.

The Vaipulya Sūtras is a work composed out of the material of the old Sūtras and has been adopted by the Mahāyānists and incorporated in their new canon.

The Mahāyāna Sūtra Sukhāvatī Vyūha or Amitāyus Sūtra is another Mahāyāna work translated into Chinese about A.D. 170.

The Tantras, esoteric in character, coincide with the decline of Buddhism.

Besides the three Piṭakas there are nine Aṅgas which are common to the Buddhists of the North and the South, although with the Northern Buddhists the enumeration of twelve kinds of *Pravacanas* is more common.

It is believed that the original language of the sacred books was not Pāli but some form of the dialect of Magadha, although Pāli has so far been shown to be the most original version. It is probable that Māgadhī was replaced by other local dialects in a transition to the Saṁskrit version of the North.

IV. THE SIX SCHOOLS OF HINDU PHILOSOPHY

THE NYĀYA SYSTEM

16. The Nyāya Philosophy.

The Nyāya System is usually considered to be a body of logical doctrines, and so it is, but we must remember that it comprehends much more than the traditional logic of the West does. There is a good deal of metaphysics and epistemology included in it, and it has that theological tinge as well, which characterises all the systems of Indian thought. In fact, theology, metaphysics and epistemology are the invariable constituents of all the Indian Systems. An investigation into the means of obtaining the 'mokṣa'—salvation or spiritual emancipation—is the common topic of all these schools of philosophy, and hence their theological aspect. This search for the means to a definitely conceived end leads the thinker to undertake a metaphysical enquiry into the nature of Being, which, in its turn, necessitates a consideration of the nature of knowledge and of the right means to acquire it.

With regard to the beginnings of the Nyāya, it may be said that we do not find any trace of the existence of these doctrines as a system either in the Vedas, or in the Brāhmaṇas, although it may be surmised that philosophical discussions, which became a prominent feature of the period of the Upaniṣads, must have been the occasion of the gradual rise and development of this kind of logical doctrine. The ancient grammarians, such as Pāṇini, Kātyāyana and Patañjali, do not mention the Nyāya as a system in their works. The fact, that

'Ānvīkṣikī,' which is the modern name of the Nyāya, denoted in the Kauṭilya Arthaśāstra only the Sāṁkhya, the Yoga, and the Cārvāka Systems, shows that the Nyāya doctrine was not existent as a system even in 300 B.C., which is supposed to be the date of the Arthaśāstra. However, we find a mention of the Nyāya principles in the medical treatise of Caraka; but unfortunately, not only is the date of Caraka uncertain, but also the very authenticity of the available text is doubtful. The Buddhistic and the Jaina literatures also yield little help in determining the origin of the Nyāya System.

The elaborated system of the Nyāya is found in the Nyāya Sūtras of Gautama, and all that we definitely know about these is that Vātsyāyana, who lived before Dignāga, probably in the second half of the fourth century, wrote a commentary on them and he quoted Sūtras from the Vaiśeṣika. He also recognised that the two systems were allied to each other in their philosophy. This together with the fact that the Buddhistic and the Jaina literatures give pretty clear evidence of the existence of the Vaiśeṣika Sūtras at about the 1st century A.D., enables us to infer, on the basis of a close affinity between the two, that the Nyāya and the Vaiśeṣika Systems grew up side by side, or in close succession, somewhere near the 1st century of the Christian era. It is improbable that there should not have been before the Sūtras any elementary works leading up to those elaborate treatises, and so we must believe that some Nyāya literature existed even before the composition of the aphorisms of Gautama.

17. The Nyāya Sūtras of Gautama.

The first of these Nyāya Sūtras forms a good index not only to the philosophy of this particular work but also to that of the Nyāya System in general. The Sūtra runs thus :—

"It is the knowledge of the real essence of the following sixteen categories that leads to the attainment of the Highest Good: (1) The means of right cognition (*Pramāṇa*); (2) The objects of cognition (*Prameya*); (3) Doubt (*Saṁśaya*); (4) Motive (*Prayojana*); (5) Example (*Dṛiṣṭānta*); (6) Theory (*Siddhānta*); (7) Factors of Reasoning or Syllogism (*Avayava*); (8) Hypothetical Reasoning (*Tarka*); (9) Demonstrative Truth (*Nirṇaya*); (10) Discussion (*Vāda*); (11) Disputation (*Jalpa*); (12) Wrangling (*Vitaṇḍā*); (13) Fallacious Reasoning or Fallacies (*Hetvābhāsa*); (14) Perversion (*Chala*); (15) Casuistry (*Jāti*); (16) The points of refutation (*Nigrahasthāna*)."*

These categories are defined and classified as follows:

1. THE MEANS OF RIGHT COGNITION are:

(*i*) Perception (*Pratyakṣa*); (*ii*) Inference (*Anumāna*); (*iii*) Analogy (*Upamāna*) and (*iv*) Testimony (*Śabda*).

(*i*) **Perception** is that cognition which is produced by the contact of the object with a sense-organ (*indriyārtha sannikarṣotpannam*); which cannot be expressed by means of words (*avyapadeśyam*); which is not erroneous (*avyabhicāri*) and which is well-defined (*vyavasāyātmakam*). For example, the cognition of a pot by its coming into contact with the organ of sight.

(*ii*) **Inference** is that cognition which is based upon perception. It is of three kinds: (*a*) That in which the effect is inferred from the cause (*Pūrvavat*); for example, from the appearance of clouds in the sky we may infer that there will be rain; (*b*) That in which the cause is

* English Translation of this Sūtra, and of several others in this section, has been adopted from Dr. Gaṅgā Nātha Jhā's English Translation of the

inferred from the effect (*Śeṣavat*), for example, we may infer that there has been rain by noticing that the current of a particular river is muddy and full ; (*c*) That in which the inference is based upon general observation (*Sāmānyatodṛiṣṭa*), for example, we infer that the sun moves, or the earth moves, or both move, from the general observation that the relative position of two objects cannot change unless one of them moves, or both of them move from the position which they occupy at a particular moment.

There has been a little difference of opinion with regard to the interpretation of these three kinds of inference. The explanation given above, however, may be taken as the one generally accepted.

(*iii*) **Analogy** is the cognition of an object through its resemblance to some object which is already known, for example, the animal called 'gavaya'—the gayal—is known by its resemblance to a cow.

(*iv*) **Testimony** is the assertion of a reliable person. According to the Bhāṣya 'a reliable person is one who possesses a direct and right knowledge of things, who is moved by a desire to make known to others a fact as he knows it, and who is fully capable of speaking of it.'

Testimony is of two kinds : (*a*) that which relates to things that are perceived (*Dṛiṣṭārtha*) and (*b*) that which relates to things that are not perceived (*Adṛiṣṭārtha*).

2. The Objects of Cognition are :

(i) Soul (*Ātman*) ; (ii) Body (*Sarīram*) ; (iii) Sense-organs (*Indriya*) ; (iv) Things (*Artha*) ; (v) Apprehension or intellect (*Buddhi*) ; (vi) Mind (*Manas*) ; (vii) Activity (*Pravṛitti*) ; (viii) Defects (*Doṣa*) ; (ix) Rebirth (*Pretya-bhāva*) ; (x) Fruition (*Phala*) ; (xi) Pain (*Dukkha*) ; and (xii) Release (*Apavarga*).

(i) **Soul** is that which has for its signs—desire, aversion, effort, pleasure, pain and cognition.

(ii) **Body** is that which is the basis of action and of the organs of sensation.

(iii) **The Sense-organs** are those of smell, taste, sight, touch, and hearing, and these are made of gross matter.

(iv) **Things** are the objects of sense. They are smell, taste, colour, touch and sound, which are respectively the qualities of earth, water, light, air and ether.

(v) **Intellect** or apprehension is that by means of which things are cognised. Intellection, apprehension and cognition are synonymous terms.

(vi) **Mind** is that which can have only one cognition at a time, or that which can attend to only one object at a time.

(vii) **Activity** is the function of mind, speech and body.

(viii) **Defects** are those which have 'urging' or 'inciting' for their distinguishing feature. The Bhāṣya explains this definition thus: "'Inciting' means causing activity. Attachment and the rest incite or cause the activity of man towards virtuous or sinful deeds; and wherever there is ignorance, there are attachment and aversion."

(ix) **Rebirth** consists in being born again.

(x) **Fruition** is that which is produced by 'activity' and 'defect.' It consists in 'the experiencing of pleasure and pain,' as every action leads to pleasure and pain. And as pleasure and pain appear only when the body, the sense-organs, the objects and apprehension are present, what is meant to be included under the term 'fruition' is pleasure and pain along with the body and the rest; so that all these constitute 'fruition,' which is a thing produced by 'activity' and 'defect' (the Bhāṣya).

(xi) **Pain** is that which is characterised by suffering.

(xii) **Final Release** is absolute freedom from pain. The Bhāṣya explains this thus: "Release is absolute freedom from that—from the aforesaid pain, *i.e.*, from birth. How is this? When there is a relinquishing of the birth that has been taken, and a non-resumption of another, this condition which is without end is known as Final Release by those who know what Final Release is."

3. Doubt is that wavering judgment in which the definite cognition of the specific character of anyone object is wanting, for example, the doubt whether a certain object is a man or the trunk of a tree.

4. Motive is that object in order to obtain which one acts.

5. Example is that with regard to which both parties, the ordinary man and the trained investigator, entertain similar ideas. The Bhāṣya offers the following explanation: "Those men are called 'ordinary' who are not above the capacities of an average man, *i.e.*, those who are not possessed of any particular superiority of intelligence, either inherently or through hard study; and the opposite of these are 'parīkṣaka'—trained investigators, so called because they are capable of carrying on the investigation of things by means of reasoning and proofs. And that object forms an Example which is understood and known by the ordinary man just as it is by the trained investigator. The purposes served by the Example are: (*a*) The contrary opinions are overthrown by being shown to be contradictory to, and incompatible with, the Example; (*b*) One's own opinions are established by being shown to be compatible with and supported by the Example; and (*c*) The Example is utilised as the corroborative instance or illustration, which is one of the essential factors of the inferential process."

'Wherever there is smoke there is fire, as in the kitchen,' this is an instance of Example.

6. THEORY OR DOCTRINE is a conviction with regard to the exact nature of a thing dealt with by philosophy. It is of four kinds :—

(i) *Doctrine common to all philosophers* (*Sarvatantra Siddhānta*), for example, such opinions as 'The olfactory organ and the rest are sense-organs'; 'Odour and the rest are the objects apprehended by means of the sense-organs'; 'Things are cognised by means of the Instruments of Cognition.'

(ii) *Doctrine peculiar to one philosophy* (*Pratitantra Siddhānta*), for example, the following doctrines are peculiar to the Sāṁkhya: 'An absolute non-entity can never come into existence'; 'An entity can never absolutely lose its existence'; 'Intelligence is unmodifiable.'

(iii) *Doctrine resting on implication* (*Adhikaraṇa Siddhānta*) is that on the knowledge or acceptance of which depends the knowledge or acceptance of another fact. For example, as the Bhāṣya says, when the fact that the cogniser is distinct from the body and the sense-organs is proved or indicated by the fact of one and the same object's being apprehended by the organs of vision and touch,—the implications are :—(*a*) That there are more sense-organs than one; (*b*) That the sense-organs operate upon particular kinds of objects; (3) That the sense-organs have their existence indicated by the apprehension of objects, etc.

(iv) *Hypothetical Doctrine* (*Abhyupagama Siddhānta*) : A fact is taken for granted as true without investigation, and then on the basis of that assumption an enquiry arises about its details. For example, it is taken for granted that sound is a substance, and on the basis of this assumption the investigation as to whether sound is eternal or non-eternal ensues.

7. Factors of Reasoning (*Avayavāḥ*).—These are five:—(*i*) Proposition (*Pratijñā*); (*ii*) Probans (*Hetu*); (*iii*) Example (*Udāharaṇa*) ; (*iv*) Reaffirmation or Application (*Upanaya*) and (*v*) Conclusion (*Nigamana*). These form the constituents of the Indian Syllogism and are defined as follows :—

(*i*) **Proposition** is that in which an assertion is made of that which is to be proved—the Probandum; for example, 'Sound is not eternal.'

(*ii*) **Probans** is that which demonstrates the 'probandum,' through its similarity or dissimilarity to an example. For instance, Sound is non-eternal, because sound has the character of being a product; and as a matter of fact everything that is a product is not eternal, as the dish, the pot, etc. (Demonstration through similarity). Again, sound is non-eternal, because it has the character of being produced, and that which does not have the character of being produced is always eternal; for example, such substances, as the soul and the like (Demonstration through dissimilarity).

(*iii*) **Example** is either (*a*) that familiar instance, which through similarity to what is to be proved, is possessed of a property of it, or (*b*) that familiar instance which, through dissimilarity to what is to be proved is not possessed of a property of it. Examples: (*a*) Sound is not eternal, because it has the character of being produced just like such things as the dish, the cup and the like; (*b*) Sound is not eternal, because it has the character of being produced, and everything not having the character of being produced is eternal, for instance, the soul and the rest.

(*iv*) **Reaffirmation or Application** is that which on the strength of the example reasserts the subject as (*a*) being 'so,' that is, as being possessed of the character which has been found in the example to be concomitant with the probandum, or (*b*) as being 'not so,' that is, as not being possessed of the character which has been found in the example to be concomitant with the negation of the probandum. "(*a*) When the example cited is a homogeneous one which is similar to the subject, for example, when a dish is cited as an example to show that sound is non-eternal, we have the reaffirmation stated in the form: 'Sound is so,' *i.e.*, 'Sound is a product,' where the character of being a product is applied to sound, the subject of thought. When the example cited is a heterogeneous one, which is dissimilar to the subject, *e.g.*, when the soul is cited as an example of a substance which not being a product is eternal, the reaffirmation is stated in the form: 'Sound is not so,' where the character of being a product is reasserted of sound through the denial of the character of not being produced." Thus there are two kinds of Reaffirmation based upon two kinds of example.

(v) **The Conclusion** is the restatement of the proposition on the basis of the statement of the probans.

" The probans having been stated either per similarity or per dissimilarity, we have a recapitulation of the entire reasoning in accordance with the example, and this recapitulation constitutes the final conclusion, which is in the form—' Therefore, having the character of product, sound is non-eternal.' This has been called 'Nigamana,' because it serves to connect or string together the proposition, the probans, the example, and the reaffirmation." —(The Bhāṣya.)

When the probans is stated per similarity, we get the following syllogism :

1. Sound is non-eternal, Proposition (Pratijñā).
2. Because it is produced ; Probans (Hetu).
3. Whatever is produced is non-eternal, as the dish, etc.; Example (Dṛiṣṭānta).
4. Sound is produced, Reaffirmation (Upanaya).
5. Therefore, it is non-eternal. Conclusion (Nigamana).

When the probans is stated per dissimilarity the syllogism is as follows:

1. Sound is non-eternal, Proposition.
2. Because it is produced ; Probans.

3.	Whatever is not produced is eternal, as the soul, etc.;	Example.
4.	Sound is not that which is not produced,	Reaffirmation.
5.	Therefore sound is non-eternal.	Conclusion.

The more familiar example of an Indian Syllogism is the following:

1.	The hill is fiery,	Proposition.
2.	Because it smokes ;	Probans.
3.	Whatever smokes is fiery, as a hearth in the kitchen ;	Example.
4.	This hill is smoking,	Reaffirmation.
5.	Therefore, it is fiery.	Conclusion.

This form of argument, consisting of five parts, is used when the aim is to convince another person of the truth of the conclusion. When one reasons for oneself, however, there are only three steps in the argument, just as we have them in the Aristotelian syllogism. It is of the following form :

1. All that smokes is fiery,
2. This hill is smoking,
3. Therefore, this hill is fiery.

We quote the following from Davies' "Hindu Philosophy" in order to explain the nature and the parts of an Indian syllogism : "The term 'Vyāpti'—'pervasion' or 'invariable concomitance'—is used to express the connection in the major premiss of the Aristotelian syllogism. Inference is defined as the knowledge which is caused by the knowledge of 'Vyāpti,' or a knowledge generable by a mediate judgment (*parāmarśa*). This mediate judgment is a recognition that there is in the subject of the question (*pakṣa*) an attribute characterised by a pervasion (or universal concomitance, ' Vyāpti'). In other words, the *subject of the question* has a property universally accompanied by something else, *viz.*, by that which is to be proved or disproved of it by the ' Sādhya ' or predicate of the conclusion."

The meaning of ' Vyāpti ' has been fully explained by Śaṁkara Miśra: "It may be asked, What is this invariable concomitance? It is not merely a relation of coextension. Nor is it the relation of totality. For if you say that invariable concomitance is the connection of the middle term with the whole of the major term, such connection does not exist in the case of smoke (for smoke does not always exist where there is fire). Nor is it natural conjunction, for the nature of a thing is the thing's proper mode of being . . . Nor is it the possession of a form determined by the same connection as something else; as for instance, the being fiery is not determined by connection with smoke, for the being fiery is more extensive. We proceed, then, to state that invariable concomitance is a connection requiring no qualifying term or limitation. It is an extensiveness coextensive with the predicate. In other words, invariable concomitance is invariable coinherence of the predicate."

The qualifying term or limitation is called *Upādhi*. Fire always underlies smoke, but smoke does not always accompany fire; and the proposition that smoke accompanies fire requires a qualifying condition (*Upādhi*)—that there must be moist fuel, which may not be present. An universal proposition is not, therefore, simply convertible, but only convertible by limitation *per accidens*. The *Upādhi* is the limitation, or qualifying condition, which is necessary for the conversion of the proposition.

The process by which the *Vyāpti* is determined is called *Vyāptigraha*, and is a generalisation by experience or induction. Induction is defined as "the determination of unconditional and of conditional concomitances." The Hindu logicians are quite aware of the necessity of a sound induction for the establishment of a universal proposition. From a passage in Muktāvali we learn that such a proposition must be proved by affirmative and negative induction, which correspond to the Methods of Agreement and Difference in Mill's Logic, the object being to discover a certain relation of cause and effect between the two phenomena. "The two suggestors of the relation of cause and effect are (1) this concomitancy of affirmatives—that whenever the product exists the material cause thereof exists; and (2) this concomitancy of negatives—that when the material cause no longer exists the product no longer exists."

8. HYPOTHETICAL REASONING is that in which, when the true character of a thing is not well-known, there is put forward, for the purpose of ascertaining that real character, a reasoning which proves a certain conclusion by showing the undesirability or absurdity of the contradictory of that conclusion. The Bhāṣya illustrates Hypothetical Reasoning as follows: "As an example of this kind of reasoning, we have the following (in regard to the cognitive soul being a product and having a beginning, or being beginningless):—First of all there arises a desire to know the real character of the cogniser, the agent who cognises what is to be cognised,—this desire being in the form 'May I know the real character of the cogniser.' Then comes the doubt in the form: Has this cogniser a beginning or is it beginningless? —thus there being a doubt with regard to the real character of the thing the enquirer accepts and assents to

that particular character in support of which he finds proofs and grounds for acceptance." The following will be the form of a hypothetical argument intended to prove that the cognitive self must be beginningless:

If it is necessary that metempsychosis and release should be possible for the cognitive self, it must be beginningless;

It is necessary that metempsychosis and release should be possible for the cognitive self,

Therefore the cognitive self must be beginningless.

9. Demonstrative Truth.—When there is an ascertainment of the real character of a thing after duly deliberating over the two sides of a question—an argument in favour of a certain conclusion, and also that in its confutation, we have what is called Demonstrative Truth or Definitive Cognition.

"Every discussion ends in showing the possibility or reasonableness of one view and the impossibility or unreasonableness of the confutation of (the arguments against) that view or *vice versa*, the reasonableness of the confutation and the unreasonableness of the original view; and it is only when we have both of these—the reasonableness and the unreasonableness—that they conjointly set aside the doubt or uncertainty attaching to the real character of the thing; while if we do not have them both, the uncertainty continues to remain."—(The Bhāṣya.)

When there is a controversy between two persons over a certain question, it takes three forms: Discussion, Disputation, and Wrangling.

10. Discussion consists in the putting forward by two persons of a conception (*pakṣa*) and counter-conception (*pratipakṣa*), in which there is supporting and condemning of these by means of proofs and reasonings, neither of which is quite opposed to the main doctrine or thesis,

and both of which are carried out in full accordance with the method of reasoning through the five factors. For example, we may have the conception 'Soul is' and its counter-conception 'Soul is not.' It is to be remembered that there is room for discussion only when the conception and the counter-conception are alleged to subsist in the same substratum.

11. DISPUTATION is that which is endowed with the characteristics of Discussion, and in which there is supporting and condemning by means of Perversion, Casuistry and the Points of Refutation. These are explained in detail in the sequel. Perversion is the opposing of an assertion through the assumption of an alternative meaning. Casuistry consists in opposing an assertion through similarity and dissimilarity. The Points of Refutation consist in the indicating of the disputant's misunderstanding and failing to understand the point at issue.

12. WRANGLING.—Disputation becomes wrangling when there is no establishing of the counter-conception, that is, when a certain party does not establish any doctrine of its own, but only criticises the proofs adduced for the establishing of the view of the opposite party.

15. FALLACIOUS REASONING is that in which the probans does not possess all the characteristics of a true probans, and yet is sufficiently similar to the true probans to appear as such. The fallacies due to a false probans are of the following kinds:—

(*i*) **Inconclusive Reasoning** (*Savyabhicāra*); (*ii*) **Contradictory Reasoning** (*Viruddha*); (*iii*) **Neutralised Reasoning** (*Prakaraṇasama*); (*iv*) **Reasoning by means of an unproved Probans** (*Sādhyasama*) and (*v*) **Belated or Mistimed Probans** (*Kālātīta*).

(*i*) **Inconclusive Reasoning** is that argument which is vitiated by indecision or uncertainty. For example, in the argument 'Sound is eternal, because it is intangible,' for tangible things, as the jar, etc., are non-iternal, we find that the character of intangibility has been put forward in order to prove the character of eternality, while, as a matter of fact, the two characters do not bear to each other the relation of proof and that which is proved, as all non-eternal things are not tangible ; for example, Intellect (*Buddhi*) is non-eternal, and yet it is intangible; and an atom, although tangible, is yet eternal. The argument will make the following Aristotelian Syllogism vitiated by the Fallacy of Undistributed Middle :

> Some intangible things are eternal (such as the soul, etc.),
> Sound is intangible,
> ∴ Sound is eternal.

(*ii*) **Contradictory Reasoning** is that argument which contradicts or sets aside an admitted fact or doctrine. The Bhāṣya cites an example from the Yogabhāṣya on the Yogasūtra III. 13. It is stated that (*i*) This world, being a modification, ceases from manifestation, because its eternality is denied, and (*ii*) Even when thus ceasing it continues to exist, because its utter destruction is denied. Here we find that the first statement is contradicted by the second in that while the one denies eternality to all that which is a modification, the other admits the possibility of the continuance of that which is a modification.

(*iii*) **Neutralised Reasoning** is that in which the probans which is put forward to establish a definite conclusion only gives rise to suspense in regard to the point at issue. For example, 'Sound is non-eternal, because we do not find in it the properties of an eternal thing; and we have found in the case of such things as the dish, etc., that what is not found to possess the properties of an eternal thing is non-eternal." The suspense in regard to this reasoning is due to the fact that the person to whom this kind of reasoning is addressed does not find in sound either such properties as are invariably concomitant with eternality, or such as are inseparable from non-eternality. The Tātparya—a commentary on the Sūtras—thus explains the difference between the Inconclusive and the Neutralised Reasoning: "The probans in the reasoning—'Sound is non-eternal, because the properties of an eternal thing are not found in it'—would be called inconclusive, only if the non-finding of the properties of an eternal thing were known to subsist in a thing which is admitted by both parties to be eternal, or the non-finding of the properties of a non-eternal thing were known to subsist in a thing admitted by both parties to be non-eternal. As it is, however, neither of these two conditions is fulfilled by the case cited, in which all that we have is that in sound there is non-finding of the properties of an eternal thing, and also the non-finding of the properties of a not-eternal thing; and as these circumstances neutralise each other, the reasoning is called 'neutralised.'"

(*iv*) **Reasoning by means of an Unproved Probans** is that in which the probans by means of which it is sought to prove the truth of a proposition (probandum) is itself unproved, and is, therefore, similar to the probandum in this respect. For example, if some one reasons 'Shadow is a substance, because it has motion,' the probans—'Because it has motion'—does not differ from the probandum —'Shadow is a substance'—inasmuch as it has itself to be proved. What has to be ascertained is the following: Does the shadow move like a man? Or is it that as the object obstructing light moves along, there is a continuity of the obstruction, which leads to the continuity of the absence of light, and it is this absence of light which is perceived as the shadow? (The Bhāṣya.)

(*v*) **Belated or Mistimed Probans** is that in which the phenomenon which is assigned as the cause is not the real cause, because it is affected by lapse of time, that is to say, it is not the cause, because it ceases to exist at the time of the production of the effect, and hence the probans is called 'belated' or 'mistimed.' For example, the argument that 'Sound is eternal because it is manifested by conjunction, like colour. The colour that is manifested by the conjunction of light with the jar is one that was in existence before, as well as after its manifestation. Similarly, the sound also that is manifested by the conjunction of the drum and the stick, or by the conjunction of the wood and the axe, is one that is in existence before and after its manifestation; so that being manifested by conjunction, sound must be regarded as eternal.' Now this is not a valid argument, for the case of the production of sound is not similar to that of the production of the sensation of colour. It is only during the time at which the conjunction of the light and the jar is present that colour is perceived, while in the case of sound it is only after the conjunction of the drum and the stick has ceased that sound is heard;—in fact it is heard at the time of disjunction. Thus the manifestation of sound is beyond the time of conjunction, and, as such, it cannot be caused by conjunction, because as a rule when the cause has ceased to exist, the effect does not appear. What is adduced as the probans in the argument is not similar to the example, and as such it cannot prove the proposition, and hence it is fallacious.

When in argumentation it is found that the reasoning is fallacious, the disputant, still trying to snatch victory for himself, makes use of what are known as Perversion and Casuistry. These are explained as follows :

14. PERVERSION is the refutation of a proposition by assigning to it a meaning other than the one intended ; for example, the proposition—'*Navakambaloyam māṇavakaḥ*,' which really means 'This boy is one who has a new blanket,' may be taken to mean 'This boy has nine blankets,'—the word '*nava*' in the compound '*navakambalaḥ*' being an ambiguous term meaning both 'nine' and 'new.'

15. CASUISTRY OR FUTILE REJOINDER is an objection taken on the basis of mere similarity or dissimilarity ; that is to say, when the probans put forward by the first party is one that is intended to prove the conclusion through its similarity to the Example, and an objection is taken on the basis of its dissimilarity to that Example ; or when the probans put forward is intended to prove the conclusion through its dissimilarity to the Example, and an objection is taken on the basis of its similarity to it.

Modern logicians have defined a Futile Rejoinder as simply '*asad uttaram*'—a wrong answer, *i.e.*, an answer which is either incapable of shaking the opposite view or vitiated by self-contradiction.

16. THE POINTS OF REFUTATION OR CLINCHERS are those cases in which the argument suffers from either 'misapprehension' or 'incomprehension.' 'Misapprehension' is that comprehension which is either wrong or reprehensible. The man who misapprehends things

becomes defeated; and Clincher consists in this defeat. It is a case of 'incomprehension' when the subject being one on which something has to be said the person engaged in discussion does not say anything; that is to say, either he does not oppose what has been sought to be proved by the other party, or does not meet the objections that may have been urged against himself.

According to the Tātparya a 'misapprehension' is called simply wrong when the subject-matter is something too subtle to be grasped by an ordinary intellect; it is called 'reprehensible' when it pertains to something gross—an ordinary topic which is within the range of ordinary minds.

There is a multiplicity of Futile Rejoinders and Clinchers, the detailed explanation of which is given in the last chapter of the Nyāya-Sūtras. It is not possible, however, to deal with these in this introductory treatise, nor are they so very important.

18. The Nyāya Metaphysics and the Doctrine of Causation.

The metaphysics of the Nyāya establishes the existence of God, matter and the individual soul as three distinct eternal entities. The soul has an inherent power of perception through the sense-organs, which include the mind also as one of them, and of making use of the other instruments of acquiring knowledge, *viz.*, of Inference, Analogy, and Revelation or Testimony. The world has been created by God out of the primordial matter, which is eternal. Salvation, which means freedom from the pains attendant upon repeated birth and death, is attainable through true knowledge, for the possession of that brings about the cessation of metempsychosis.

Before closing this exposition of the Nyāya system it is important to explain briefly the doctrine of causation as it is usually accepted by the Nyāya philosophers. The Nyāya view of causation is known as the 'Asatkāryavāda,' that is to say, the doctrine that the effect does not exist in the cause beforehand, but that it is produced out of it by the conjunction of certain conditions. This doctrine is the opposite of the 'Satkāryavāda' of the Sāṁkhya, which implies that the effect is already present in the cause and, therefore, the effect is only another form of the cause. This latter view is based upon the principle that nothing which is existent is ever non-existent (*Nabhāvo vidyate sataḥ*), and that nothing which is non-existent is ever existent (*Nasato vidyate bhāvaḥ*).

According to the Nyāya, a cause is that invariable antecedent condition which is not proved to be an unessential and accidental circumstance.

An accidental circumstance (*Anyathāsiddhi*) is of three kinds: (*i*) Anything which happens to be conjoined with such conditions as are found to be adequate to produce the effect by themselves. For example, the presence of an ass, at the time of the production of a particular jar, is an accidental circumstance; while the clay, the potter's wheel, the rod, and the potter himself constitute the real cause; (*ii*) Anything which although an invariable antecedent of a certain effect is also an invariable and necessary antecedent of an effect different from the one in question. For example, the presence of ether (*ākāśa*) is an accidental circumstance attendant upon the production of a jar, for it is known to be the essential and invariable condition of another effect, sound; (*iii*) Anything which is necessarily apprehended with the real cause of an effect—for example, threadness and the form of threads are accidental circumstances attendant upon the production of a piece of cloth, for they are apprehended along with the threads which form the real cause of the piece of cloth.

An effect is that which necessarily follows such invariably concomitant conditions as cannot be proved to be unessential and accidental circumstances.

Causes are of three kinds : (*i*) The Inherent Cause (*Samavāyi-kāraṇa*) ; (*ii*) The Non-inherent Cause (*Asamavāyi-kāraṇa*) and (*iii*) The Instrumental Cause (*Nimitta-kāraṇa*). These are explained as follows:—

(*i*) The Inherent Cause is that which stands in intimate relation (*Samavāya-sambandha*) to its effect. Intimate relation means inseparable connection (*Ayuta-sambandha*). For example, threads are the inherent cause of a piece of cloth, and a piece of cloth is the inherent cause of its colour.

(*ii*) The Non-inherent Cause is that which is proximate to the inherent cause of an effect. For example, the conjunction of yarn is the non-inherent cause of a piece of cloth, for it stands in proximate relation to yarn which is the inherent cause of cloth. Similarly, the colour of the threads is indirectly the non-inherent cause of the colour of a piece of cloth, for the colour of the threads stands in intimate relation to the threads, the threads stand in intimate relation to the piece of cloth, and the piece of cloth is the inherent cause of its own colour.

(*iii*) The Instrumental Cause is defined as one which includes all such causes as cannot be brought under either of the two preceding heads. For example, the potter's rod and the wheel are instrumental causes of a jar. Similarly, the shuttle and the weaver are instrumental causes of a piece of cloth.

19. The Nyāya Literature.

We can trace a regular development of the Nyāya literature after the Nyāya Sūtras through the works of Uddyotakara, Vācaspati Miśra, Bhāsarvajña, Udayana, and Śrīdhara, who all belonged to what has come to be known as the Old School of Nyāya.

The New School of Indian Logic (*Navya-nyāya*) was founded by the great Bengali logician Gaṅgeśa. This school is also known as the Nuddea School of Logic. The successors of Gaṅgeśa were Jayadeva, Vardhamāna, Jagadīśa and Śaṁkara Miśra. The doctrines of the New School are based upon the Tattvacintāmaṇi of Gaṅgeśa, and they are characterised by abstruse thought and terminology devoting themselves mainly to a discussion of the theory of knowledge. This school began somewhere between 1150 and 1200 A.D., and went on developing up to about 1600 A.D.

Then followed a third school of Syncretistic Logicians, who tried to combine the old and the new systems. Śivāditya, Keśava Miśra, Laugākṣi Bhāskara, Annambhaṭṭa, and Varadācārya belong to this school. The latest book on Nyāya—the Nīlakaṇṭhī of Nīlakaṇṭha, was written as late as 1840 A.D., although it is not a very important work.

In the mediæval age the Jainas and the Buddhists developed an independent system of Logic which was confined to the discussion of strictly logical problems. In connection with Jaina Logic the works of Bhadra Bāhu (357 B.C.), Umāsvāti, Siddhasena Divākara (537 A.D.),

Māṇikya Nandī (800 A.D.), Deva Sūri (1159 A.D.) and Prabhācandra are worthy of mention. Dignāga's Pramāṇasamuccaya and Nyāya Praveśa (500 A.D) and Dharmakīrti's Pramāṇavārtika-kārikā and Nyāya-bindu (650 A.D.) are important works in the school of Buddhistic Logic. It was Dignāga's criticism of the Hindu Logic in his Pramāṇasamuccaya that prompted Uddyotakara to write his Vārtika on the Vātsyāyana Bhāṣya.

THE VAIŚEṢIKA SYSTEM

20. Introductory.

After what has been said about the Nyāya System much need not be said about the Vaiśeṣika. There is nothing very peculiar in it except that it is a fuller development of the atomic theory which is also to be found in the Nyāya system. In the Vaiśeṣika the categories, the knowledge of which leads to the attainment of the *summum bonum*, are six, and according to some writers, they are seven. They are substance, attribute, action, generality, particularity, inhesion or inseparability, and, according to some, privation or negation. These, we can easily notice, are much nearer to the Aristotelian Categories than the sixteen *Padārthas* of Gautama. Further, the Vaiśeṣika system admits only two methods of proof, *viz.*, perception and inference. The arrangement of the objects of knowledge is also different from that of the Nyāya.

The chief work of the Vaiśeṣika system of philosophy is the Vaiśeṣika Sūtras, which are believed to have been composed by the sage Kaṇāda. The age of this work has already been shown to have been somewhere near the first century after Christ. There is no such important development of the system as we find in the case of the Nyāya. The reason for this may be found in the fact that there is nothing very peculiar and important in the system to distinguish it from the allied doctrine of the Nyāya, and hence it did not attract much attention. The commentary of Praśastapāda on the Vaiśeṣika Sūtras, however, shows a good deal of originality and may be taken by itself as an important addition to the Vaiśeṣika literature.

21. Outlines of the Vaiśeṣika Philosophy.

The fourth aphorism of the Vaiśeṣika Sūtras introduces the philosophy of the system as follows :—

"The highest good results from knowledge of the truth which springs from particular merit and is obtained by means of the similarity and dissimilarity of the categories (which are) Substance (*Dravya*); Attribute (*Guṇa*); Action (*Karma*); Generality (*Sāmānya*); Particularity (*Viśeṣa*); Inhesion (*Samavāya*)."

It may be pointed out that this system is called 'Vaiśeṣika' after the name of the fifth category 'Viśeṣa' which receives special treatment.

It is also to be noted that in the Vaiśeṣika Sūtras only six categories are recognised, and that the seventh category of 'Negation' or 'Privation' (*Abhāva*) was added later on.

The various categories are explained as follows :

(1) **Substance** is that which has some attribute or quality. There are nine substances, *viz.*, Earth (*Pṛithivī*); Water (*Apas*); Light (*Tejas*); Air (*Vāyu*); Ether (*Ākāśa*); Time (*Kāla*); Space (*Dik*); Soul (*Ātman*); and the Internal Organ or Mind (*Manas*).

Of these earth, water, light, air and mind are said to be made of atoms, which are extremely minute, invisible, indivisible and eternal particles of matter. Each of them has a specific differentia, and particular kinds of atoms form particular kinds of substances. A combination of two atoms is called '*Dvy-aṇuka*,' and an aggregate of three of them is called '*Trasa-reṇu*,' which is the minutest visible form of matter. The combination and dissolution of atoms is supposed to take place through an unseen peculiar force called '*adṛiṣṭa*.' This mysterious force, according to the author of the Vaiśeṣika Sūtras, does not seem to be anything more than a peculiar inherent quality of the atoms themselves. In the opinion of his followers, however, it represents the power of God or the Supreme Spirit.

(2) **Attribute or Quality** is that which is found in some substance. There are seventeen qualities:—Colour (*rūpa*); Taste (*rasa*); Smell (*gandha*); Touch (*sparśa*); Number (*saṁkhyā*); Dimensions (*parimāṇa*); Individuality (*pṛithaktva*); Conjunction (*saṁyoga*); Disjunction (*vibhāga*); Priority (*paratva*); Posteriority (*aparatva*); Cognitions (*buddhayaḥ*); Pleasure (*sukha*); Pain (*duḥkha*); Desire (*icchā*); Aversion (*dveṣa*); Volition (*prayatna*).

To these seventeen qualities seven more were added by the followers of Kaṇāda. These are: Gravity (*gurutva*); Fluidity (*dravatva*); Viscidity (*sneha*); Intellection (*buddhi*); Sound (*śabda*); Merit (*dharma*); Demerit (*adharma*).

(3) **Action** is of five kinds:—motion upwards; motion downwards; contraction, expansion and motion in general.

(4) **Generality or Universality** is the notion of a class—of a genus or a species—or of the sameness among the members of a class. The highest genus is called *parajāti*, and it is the notion of 'existence' or 'being.' The intermediate genera or species are called '*aparajāti*.' Generality is supposed to have an independent existence, although it is found also in substance, attribute and action. It is also eternal.

(5) **Particularity** is the notion of the individuality of things—*viz.*, of that which distinguishes one entity from another. It is applicable to soul, mind, time, place, the ethereal element and atoms.

(6) **Inhesion** is the notion of an inseparable connection of things, such as that of yarn and the piece of cloth prepared out of it.

(7) **Negation or Privation** is of two kinds: (*i*) Universal Negation and (*ii*) Mutual Negation.

(*i*) **Universal Negation** is subdivided under three heads:

(*a*) *Antecedent Negation*—a negation at the present time of that which will come into existence at some time in the future. For example, the negation of cloth in the yarn out of which it is to be prepared.

(*b*) *Emergent Negation*—the negation of some thing after it is destroyed or after it has ceased to exist. For example, the negation of a jar after it is broken.

(*c*) *Mutual Negation* is the reciprocal absence of the identity of one thing in another. For example, the absence of cloth in a jar and *vice versa*.

It has already been pointed out that there is hardly any remarkable development in the Vaiśeṣika literature after the Vaiśeṣika Sūtras of Kaṇāda. Besides the first commentary of Praśastapāda on the Sūtras, which certainly can claim some originality, we have a number of commentaries on the Praśastapāda. These are Vyomavatī by Vyomaśekharācārya; Nyāyakandalī by Śrīdhara; Kiraṇāvalī by Udayana; Līlāvatī by Śrīvatsācārya; Bhāṣyasūkti by Jagadīśa Bhaṭṭācārya and Kaṇādarahasya by Śaṁkara Miśra. Śaṁkara Miśra also wrote an independent commentary on the Vaiśeṣika Sūtras called the Upaskāra.

THE SĀMKHYA SYSTEM

22. The Sāṁkhya Doctrines.

In order to appreciate adequately the account of the origin and development of the system it is necessary that one should know first in outline the main doctrines which it represents. Therefore, before entering into a discussion of chronological details, I should like to state briefly the essential principles of the Sāṁkhya system of philosophy.

The name of the system—'Sāṁkhya'—is derived from the Saṁskṛit word '*saṁkhyā*,' which usually means 'number,' 'calculation' or 'enumeration,' and sometimes it also signifies 'discrimination,' 'reasoning,' or 'deliberation.' Now both these meanings of 'saṁkhyā' indicate happily the essential nature of the Sāṁkhya Philosophy, for this system does aim at calculating or enumerating the true principles, or better, the essential elements of Reality, technically called the *Tattvas* dna at employing, more than any other system does, the purely rationalistic method of exposition.

In order to present the doctrine of the Sāṁkhya in outline, and in a form in which it is most familiar I shall draw upon the subject-matter of the Sāṁkhya Kārikâ of Īśvara Kṛiṣṇa, which beyond doubt occupies the most important position in the history of Sāṁkhya literature for the simple reason that it represents the system at a stage of development when it had just emerged from the confusion and obscurity of the embryonic state, and, is the same time, had not yet been contaminated by coming into contact with other philosophic influences.

The Aim of Philosophy.—The Sāṁkhya Kārikā begins by pointing out that the aim of all enquiry is the removal of the three kinds of pain to which man is liable in his earthly existence. These are :

(*i*) The Naturo-intrinsic (*Ādhyātmika*)—the physical and mental pain due to purely internal causes, such as disease, anguish, etc.

(*ii*) The Naturo-extrinsic (*Ādhibhautika*)—the pain due to exclusively external causes in nature.

(*iii*) The pain due to the influence of supernatural causes, such as gods, demons, etc. (*Ādhidaivika*).

The next step is to discuss the means of alleviating this threefold suffering. And, here, in keeping with the characteristic spirit of the true Sāṁkhya, it is emphatically pointed out that the discriminative or the rationalistic method of enquiry is the only sound one. For it is only this procedure which puts an end to all pain by enabling a man to acquire true knowledge, which consists of a right understanding of the nature of the *Avyakta*—the unmanifested, and the *Vyakta*—the manifested Reality.

The Sāṁkhya Categories, which are really the various constituent elements of Being, may be classified under the following heads :—

(*i*) That which is only a cause and not an effect.

(*ii*) That which is both a cause and an effect.

(*iii*) That which is only an effect and not a cause.

(*iv*) That which is neither a cause nor an effect.

Now the various elements of reality are distributed among the four classes as follows :—

(*a*) *The Unmanifested Nature or the Primordial Matter* (*prakṛiti* or *pradhāna*) is the ultimate cause of the whole material universe and is itself without a cause. Thus it is purely productive.

(*b*) The Great Element (*mahat*), which is a name for the intellect (*buddhi*), is produced out of the Unmanifested Primordial Matter.

(*c*) Egoism or self-consciousness (*ahaṁkāra*) is the product of the Intellect.

(*d*) The Five Subtle Elements (*pañca-tanmātrāṇi*) are produced out of the Principle of Egoism and are the primary forms of all manifested Reality.

Thus the seven elements mentioned under (b), (c) *and* (d) *are both causes and effects.*

(*e*) The Five Gross Elements (*pañca-mahābhūtāni*), *viz.*, earth, water, fire or light, air and ether, which arise out of the five Subtle Elements.

(*f*) The Five Organs of Sense (*pañca-jñānendriyāṇi*), *viz.*, the eye, the nose, the tongue, the ear and the skin.

(*g*) The Five Organs of Action (*pañca-karmendriyāṇi*), *viz.*, the voice, the hands, the feet, the anus and the organs of generation.

(*h*) The Receptive and the Discriminating Faculty (*manas*).

These eleven—the five organs of sense, the five organs of action and the *manas*—are produced out of Egoism or self-consciousness, and do not produce anything. Thus they, together with the five gross elements, *are only effects.*

(*i*) Spirit (*puruṣa*) is neither the cause nor the effect of anything.

Thus there are twenty-five principles in the universe:—

Primordial Matter	...	...	...	1
Intellect ...	...	...	...	1
Egoism or Self-consciousness		..	...	
The Subtle Elements ...		..	...	
The Gross Elements	...	...	...	5
The Organs of Sense	...	...	...	5
The Organs of Action	..	...	...	5
Manas or the Discriminative Faculty			...	1
Spirit ...		...	...	1
		Total	...	25

The principles of *Buddhi* and *Ahaṁkāra*, which have been translated generally into English as 'Intellect' or 'Will' and 'Egoism,' may be better rendered by 'consciousness' and 'self-consciousness' respectively. Similarly, the term 'manas' as used in the Sāṁkhya does not mean what we usually understand by 'mind.' It has the more restricted sense of 'imagination' or 'ideation,' or both—*saṁkalpakamatra manaḥ iti*; *idamevaṁ, naivam iti samyak kalpayati, viśeṣaṇa viśeṣya bhāvena vivecayatīti yāvat*, that is to say, 'it is the reflecting principle'; it is the principle which supplies forms and qualifications to the abstract cognition of a certain object, which invariably precedes the concrete and well-defined knowledge thereof.

Then what is meant by these terms is not so much the psychical states as the physical organs, for all of them are evolved out of matter.

The principle of spirit has reference, at least in the later Sāṁkhya, to individual spirits only. For, the universal or the supreme spirit has no place in this system, and for this reason it has been called an atheistic or godless philosophy.

The Doctrine of the Guṇas.—The next important point in the cosmogony of the Sāṁkhya is the doctrine of the three 'Guṇas' (literally, qualities) which are supposed to be the constituents of the Primordial Matter. These are Goodness (*sattva*); Passion or Foulness (*rajas*); and Darkness (*tamas*). Goodness is considered as light or subtle and enlightening or manifesting; Passion or Foulness as exciting and mobile; and Darkness as heavy and enveloping or obstructive. It is through the combined functions of these constituent modes of *prakṛiti* (matter) that the various forms of the manifested universe are evolved. In the unmanifested state of nature these modes are in a state of equilibrium. Through an unaccountable factor motion, or better commotion, is introduced into Nature and it is *rajas*—the mode of Passion or Foulness which is set in action first. This activity turns the unmanifested into the twenty-three various forms of the manifested in the order shown above in the enumeration of the Sāṁkhya Categories. The three constituents of Nature enter into the formation of each of these forms, and differences in the nature of classes and individual things are explained by the differences of the presence or absence of these modes, or by those of the proportion in which they happen to be combined in their constitution. For example, Goodness (*sattva*), which is characterised by luminousness (*prakāśa*), is prevalent in fire; Passion (*rajas*), which represents activity (*pravṛitti*), predominates in air; and Darkness (*tamas*), which stands for dullness (*moha*), is the chief element in earth, which being heavy, is supposed to be formed by, and to represent the gross stupefying element. The same three *guṇas* explain respectively the three distinct properties of pleasure, pain and insensibility. Lightness and heaviness; light and darkness; knowledge and ignorance; intelligence and dullness are explained by Goodness and Darkness respectively; activity and inactivity by Passion and Darkness. In a word, both the physical and the psychical (including the moral) qualities are supposed to be determined by these three modes of Nature. It would be extremely interesting and instructive to study in greater detail how the various principles and the multifarious forms of reality are evolved and what their nature and function exactly are, but the limits of this treatise can hardly admit of any further discussion of the subject. However, it is essential to consider briefly the character of Spirit and its relation to Nature.

The Relation between Spirit and Nature.—According to the Sāṁkhya there is a plurality of spirits, and these are totally distinct from Nature. Spirit is the subject (witness), individual, conscious, inactive and has emancipation for its goal. Nature has evolved itself into the various forms, as it were, out of sympathy with Spirit, so that by witnessing it the spirit may witness its own character and may thus, by attaining true knowledge, achieve emancipation. It is the contact of Spirit and Nature in the body which makes Spirit appear active, although in itself it is inactive, and the body conscious although it is without consciousness in its own nature. Perception is not due to the activity of spirit but to that of the Intellect (*buddhi*). Spirit is like a mirror in which through the activity of the Intellect the objects of experience are reflected and are thereby perceived. Like the mirror Spirit remains passive and unaffected, although it appears, even to itself, to be otherwise.

The Identity of Cause and Effect.—In order to prove the existence of the Unmanifested Nature—the *prakṛiti* or *pradhāna*—as the Sāṁkhya calls it, it is maintained that *the effect always resides in the cause; or rather, that there is an identity of cause and effect.* Now, as everything, except the ultimate cause, must have a cause, and as the cause is simply a latent condition of the effect, the Manifested Nature must have for its cause an unmanifested condition of it, which is the *prakṛiti* or *pradhāna*.

The Sāṁkhya Theory of Knowledge.—So much for the metaphysics of the Sāṁkhya. With regard to its theory of knowledge it has already been pointed out that according to this system all cognition is due to the activity of the Intellect and the Discriminative Faculty (*manas*), which receive impressions through the sense-organs and present them to Spirit or Self, in the intelligence or consciousness of which they are reflected as in a mirror and thus cognised. As for the proofs of knowledge or truth the Sāṁkhya recognises only three—*viz.*, Perception, Inference and Valid Testimony, and maintains that the rest, for example, Analogy, Apparent Inconsistency (*arthāpatti*) and Negation (*abhāva*) are included in those three. Without going into a detailed exposition of the three criteria of truth, I would like to point out that in spite of the claim that it adopts a purely rationalistic method of enquiry the Sāṁkhya has found a place for valid testimony, and the commentary of Vācaspati Miśra on the Kārikā, which deals with it, shows clearly that valid testimony, at least according to him, has direct reference to the authority of the Vedas and other important scriptures. Valid testimony is defined as 'true revelation' (*āpta vacanam*)—'*āpta śrutirāptavacanaṁ tu.*' Then maintaining the self-evident nature of this, writes Vācaspati Miśra—'And this is self-evident. It is true, for it, as proceeding from the superhuman Veda, is free from all doubts and defects. Similarly, all knowledge, which proceeds from the Smṛitis, the Legend and the Purāṇas founded upon the authority of Veda, is also true.'

To be fair to the author of the Sāṁkhya Kārikā as a consistent exponent of the Sāṁkhya we may admit the possibility of interpreting his Valid Testimony in the ordinary logical sense, but this note by a standard commentator like Vācaspati Miśra should be a sufficient indication of the fact that in his times the Sāṁkhya was not regarded as a purely rationalistic doctrine— that is, as one independent of the authority of 'Śruti,' 'Smṛiti,' or even of 'Purāṇa.'

Bondage and Emancipation.—Emancipation from the cycles of metempsychosis, which is the goal of all philosophy, is attained by acquiring true knowledge of the unmanifested and the manifested Nature and of Spirit so as to be able to discriminate between Nature and Spirit. The cause of bondage is the notion on the part of Spirit, due to false knowledge, that the various forms of activity and feeling belong to it; and as soon as it dissociates itself from them consequently upon a true knowledge of its own nature, and sees that they belong to Nature as represented in its physical constitution—it becomes entitled to freedom and is actually liberated immediately after the first dissolution of the body following the Enlightenment.

Such in substance is the philosophy of the Sāṁkhya. We have confined ourselves here to a mere statement of it in outline, although a careful study of it is sure to provoke comment and criticism. The study is the most fascinating from the metaphysical point of view, not because the Sāṁkhya doctrines are necessarily sound, but because they suggest some most fertile lines of thought.

23. The Origin and Growth of the Sāṁkhya System and the Sāṁkhya Literature.

To come to the origin and growth of this system, it may be pointed out that it is known to have been founded by the sage Kapila, and the Sāṁkhya Sūtras are also attributed to him. That Kapila, who is certainly believed to have lived in a remote age, cannot be the author of the Sāṁkhya Sūtras is now an established fact with all Saṁskṛit scholars. For the date of the Sūtras cannot be fixed earlier than the 14th Century A.D. The first commentator on the Sūtras was Aniruddha, who lived in the 15th Century A.D., and no other work, not excluding the Sarvadarśana-saṁgraha (about the 14th Century A.D.), refers to the Sūtras. Great ambiguity and mystery surround the name of Kapila, for, in the first instance, Kapila is said to be a divine being—"a son of Brahman, the creative form of Brahman, an incarnation of Viṣṇu, or a form of Agni, though born of Vitatha and Devahutī; one of the great ṛishis or ancient sages; a descendant of the great law-giver Manu; and to have been endowed with knowledge, virtue, freedom from passion and supernatural power at the time of his birth."* Some have

* J. Davies : Hindu Philosophy, p. 5.

identified the name with that of the sage Kapila, after whom Kapilavastu, the birthplace of Gautama Buddha, was named. The name is mentioned in the Bhagavadgītā, the Rāmāyaṇa, the Mahābhārata and the Padma Purāṇa.

These varied references hardly enable us to fix the date of Kapila and so of the systematic foundation of the Sāṁkhya doctrine. They only show that Kapila was one of the most ancient and respected teachers of the Sāṁkhya, and probably the compiler of the Sāṁkhya Sūtras attributed them to him, not because he was their actual author, but because they embodied the doctrines of which he was the time-honoured founder. I am inclined to think that he was one of the many sages of the Vedic times, and was known to teach the doctrine which in course of time came to be called the Sāṁkhya Philosophy.

Sāṁkhya in the Upaniṣads.—However, while trying to trace the origin of the Sāṁkhya doctrines we must remember what was said with regard to the general nature of the origin of all Indian philosophical systems. With regard to the peculiarities of the Sāṁkhya, *viz.*, the doctrine of the Primordial Matter (*pradhāna*) with its three constituent qualities of Goodness, Passion and Darkness; the plurality of spirits and their relation to Nature (*prakṛiti*) and the elimination of God or Brahman, it may be said that although a vague and scattered mention of them may be recognised in a verse or two of the Vedas, and in some of the earlier Upaniṣads, there is nothing in them to make us believe that they contain any such definite doctrine as that of the pure Sāṁkhya. A distinct indication of the Sāṁkhya doctrine of the 'prakṛiti' and the 'puruṣa' is to be found in the fifth verse of Chapter IV of the Śvetāśvatara Upaniṣad which runs as follows :

Ajāmekāṁ lohita śukla kṛiṣṇāṁ bahvīḥ prajāḥ sṛijamānāṁ svarūpāḥ,
Ajo hyeko juṣamāṇo' nuśete jahātyenāṁ bhuktabhogāmajo'nyaḥ,

which has been thus translated into English:

> "The one she-goat red, white, and black,
> Produceth many young, like-formed unto her,
> The one he-goat in love enjoyeth her,
> The other leaveth her whom he hath enjoyed."

We here reproduce the observations of Dr. Keith on this verse in order to explain its implications: "The passage is discussed by Śaṁkara, who seeks to see in the three colours a reference to the three colours mentioned in the Chāndogya Upaniṣad (vi. 4.) as those of the three elements there mentioned, fire, water and earth, which are produced from the Absolute and which are present in all that exists .... But the passage must obviously also be admitted to have clear traces of what is the later Sāṁkhya doctrine: the imagery of the many he-goats, and the relation of enjoyment followed by relinquishment, is precisely parallel to the similes which are often used in the classical Sāṁkhya to illustrate the relation of Spirit and Nature. Moreover, the she-goat is named 'aja' which denotes also the unborn, a fact which exactly coincides with the Sāṁkhya conception that the first principle of nature is not a product. The Sāṁkhya conception of the all-pervading character of the *Guṇas*, which in diverse measure are present in all the products of Nature, is as well suited to the description of the progeny of the goat as the view of the Chāndogya." (The Sāṁkhya System.)

A still more definite indication of the Sāṁkhya doctrine of the three *Guṇas* is to be found in the Maitrāyaṇi Upanisad, where they are distinctly called by the name of 'Sattva,' 'Rajas,' and 'Tamas,' although the philosophy of the Upaniṣad as a whole cannot be identified with the atheism of the Sāṁkhya.

A study of the Upaniṣads shows that in some of them there are already present the germs of the Sāṁkhya doctrine of the *prakṛiti* and its three constituent attributes, and also of the relation of Spirit and *prakṛiti*, but the evidence of the conception of one universal supreme Spirit is too conspicuous to allow us to recognise in the Upaniṣad any such godless dualistic system of philosophy as the pure Sāṁkhya is supposed to be. That reference to the Sāṁkhya is to be found in the Mahābhārata is true, but it is equally true that the Sāṁkhya of the Mahābhārata is not quite the same as the later atheistic doctrine which goes by that name.

Kapila, Āśuri, Pañcaśikha and Īśvarakṛiṣṇa.—To fall in now with the chronological order of the teachers of the Sāṁkhya and their works, it may be noticed that the most conspicuous names are those of Kapila, Āsuri, Pañcaśikha and Īśvarakṛiṣṇa. These are referred to by Vācaspati Miśra in the opening verse of his Sāṁkhya-tattva-kaumudī, Āsuri being mentioned as a disciple of Kapila. As already pointed out, a veil of mystery surrouuds the name of Kapila, and nothing definite can be said with regard to his life and works. All that we can infer from the references to his name is that he was probably the first great teacher of the Sāṁkhya. There are references in the later Sāṁkhya works to a treatise called the 'Ṣaṣṭhitantra' [literally, a doctrine of sixty (principles)], which is supposed to be the oldest work on the Sāṁkhya—if it was a work at all. The surmise is that it perhaps embodied the teachings of Kapila, which were later on popularised by his disciple Āsuri. Following Āsuri in succession Pañcaśikha seems to have modified the original doctrine of Kapila, which, it is believed, was not expressly atheistic, and to have divided it into many parts.

The Sāṁkhya of Caraka.—Before we pass on to Īśvarakṛiṣṇa and his Sāṁkhya Kārikā we have to take note of the doctrine as represented by Caraka (78 A.D.) who belonged to the earlier school of the Sāṁkhya. Attention has recently been drawn to this author as an exponent of the Sāṁkhya by Prof. Das Gupta, from whose History of Indian Philosophy I quote the following summary of the Sāṁkhya doctrine as given by Caraka, with a view to bringing out the salient points of the earlier school of the Sāṁkhya:

"1. *Puruṣa* is the state of *Avyakta*. 2. By a conglomeration of this *Avyakta* with its later products a conglomeration is formed which generates the so-called living being. 3. The *Tanmātrās* are not mentioned. 4. *Rajas* and *Tamas* represent the bad states of the mind and *Sattva* the good ones. 5. The ultimate state of emancipation is either absolute annihilation or characterless absolute existence, and it is spoken of as the Brahman state; there is no consciousness in this state, for consciousness is due to the conglomeration of the self with its evolutes—*buddhi*, *ahaṁkāra*, etc. 6. The senses are formed of matter (*bhautika*)."

The Earlier School of the Sāṁkhya.—The above doctrine bears a resemblance to the one attributed to Pañcaśikha in the Mahābhārata, and is essentially different from that sketched in the Sāṁkhya Kārikā of Īśvarakṛiṣṇa and in the Sāṁkhya Sūtras. So considering that there was a successive continuity of doctrine from Kapila to Caraka we may safely conclude that Kapila, Āsuri, Pañcaśikha and Caraka represented what we may call the Earlier School of the Sāṁkhya—a school which had not yet shaken off the Upaniṣadic doctrine of Brahman as the Absolute.

The Later School of the Sāṁkhya.—With the advent of Īśvarakṛiṣṇa and his Sāṁkhya Kārikā, which was written about 200 A.D., we come to what we may call the Later School of Sāṁkhya Philosophy. The doctrines as represented by the Kārikā have already been stated. Gauḍapāda, Rāja and Vācaspati Miśra (9th Century A.D.) wrote commentaries on the Kārikā, and Nārāyaṇatīrtha wrote a further commentary—Candrikā on Gauḍapāda's commentary. Gauḍapāda's and Vācaspati's commentaries are by themselves important contributions to the Sāṁkhya literature.

The next important work—the Sāṁkhya Sūtras—was compiled by some unknown author about the 13th or 14th Century A.D., and is a complete, systematic exposition of the Sāṁkhya. The doctrine of the Sūtras is practically the same as that of the Kārikā of Īśvarakṛiṣṇa. The most prominent commentator on the Sāṁkhya Sūtras was Vijñāna Bhikṣu. From his commentary Sāṁkhyapravacanabhāṣya it appears he believed that the Sāṁkhya is not necessarily an atheistic doctrine, and that in several respects he differs in his estimation of the Sāṁkhya philosophy from Vācaspati Miśra—the commentator of the Sāṁkhya Kārikā. The chief contribution of Bhikṣu is his rational explanation of the three *guṇas*, the true character of which was never explained by either Vācaspati Miśra or Gauḍapāda. Bhikṣu first pointed out that they are not mere qualities but real 'super-subtle' substances. He wrote also a brief treatise on Sāṁkhya known as the Sāṁkhyasāra. Another commentator on the Sāṁkhya Sūtras, and the first of all, was Aniruddha, who lived in the latter half of the 15th Century A.D.

Tattva Samāsa is another work, which Professor Max Müller considers to be one of a very early date, but which now is supposed by almost all the recent scholars to belong to about the 14th Century A.D. It is, as the name itself denotes, a compendium of the Sāṁkhya doctrines.

Sāṁkhya-tattva-vivecana by Sīmānanda and Sāṁkhya-tattva-yathārtha-dīpana by Bhāvāgaṇeśa are other works of some importance, both of them being written after Vijñāna Bhikṣu's commentary and his Sāṁkhya-sāra.

Sāṁkhya and Buddhism.—Such in brief are the doctrines, the origin and development of the Sāṁkhya Philosophy. A comparative study of the Sāṁkhya and Buddhism reveals remarkable similarities between the two. It is not possible here to enter into the details of a comparison between the two systems of Philosophy. It may be pointed out, however, that on the basis of this similarity of doctrine it has been supposed by some scholars that one of the two systems may have been derived from the other. The question whether one system was really the source of the other or not is full of difficulties and requires a very careful treatment.

Another doctrine allied to that of the Sāṁkhya is the Yoga Philosophy, which we shall consider in the next section.

THE YOGA SYSTEM

24. Outlines of the Yoga Philosophy.

The Yoga System of Philosophy has been called the Theistic Sāṁkhya because of its close affinity to the Sāṁkhya. The chief difference between the two is that while the pure Sāṁkhya is atheistic, that is, has no place for God, the Yoga Philosophy, while adopting the twenty-five principles of the Sāṁkhya, adds one more, that of God. The reason for this addition in the Yoga System is to be found in an attempt to find an explanation for the original impulse—the primary movement, which sets the primordial matter acting. It was hard to understand how the equilibrium of the three qualities (*guṇas*) in the unmanifested state of nature could be disturbed without an external force, or how the non-intelligent matter (*prakṛiti*) could be evolved into a harmonious and orderly universe without the activity of an intelligent being. Such a primary and intelligent force was found in God (*Iśvara*).

To come to a little more detailed exposition of the Yoga doctrine, it may be pointed out that the word 'yoga' is derived from the Saṁskṛit root 'yuj,' which means concentration (*samādhi*), and this etymological meaning of the term is a good index to the subject-matter of the Yoga Philosophy. It does not aim so much at presenting a systematic exposition of metaphysical doctrines as at formulating an elaborate method of concentration, which, according to it, is an essential factor in bringing about the liberation of the individual soul. Such is the yoga, as it is represented at least in the most authentic and elaborate treatise called the Yoga Sūtras of Patañjali and other works on Yoga proper. In the Bhagavadgītā the term 'yoga' has been used in a wider and more general sense of 'application,' meaning thereby not necessarily 'abstract concentration', but also 'undivided attention' to any work that one might undertake to do. At one place in the Gītā, Yoga has been defined as 'skill in work' —*yogaḥ karmasu kauśalam.* Some think that it is possible to interpret 'yoga' in this sense, if we take it as derived from another root '*yujir yoge.*' However, a little consideration will show that both the meanings are the same ultimately and point to some kind of concentration.

As pointed out already, according to the Sāṁkhya Philosophy, the attainment of true knowledge, which consists of seeing the difference between 'matter' and 'spirit,' leads to liberation. According to the Yoga, however, the mere arising of such knowledge cannot be sufficient for the achievement of salvation. The established psychical tendencies (the *saṁskāras* and the *vāsanās*) should be destroyed first by means of a regular and graded practice, for it is they which are the cause of the cycles of birth and death. When they are destroyed, and only when they are destroyed, must the bondage of the body necessarily disappear. These tendencies are the result of past actions, which are either (1) White (*śukla*)—that is, those which are good and produce happiness; (2) Black (*kṛiṣṇa*)—those which produce sorrow; (3) White and black (*śukla-kṛiṣṇa*)— those of a mixed nature, that is, partly good and partly bad, which are the cause of both happiness and sorrow; or (4) Neither white nor black (*Aśuklakṛiṣṇa*)—neither good nor bad, those productive of neither happiness nor sorrow. These actions, in their turn, are the result of five kinds of 'affliction' (the *kleśas*), *viz.*, (i) the false notion that intelligence belongs to intellect (*buddhi*), and that intellect is a permanent entity leading to happiness—the *Avidyā*; (ii) the notion that worldly objects and experiences really belong to our self—the *Asmitā*; (iii) the consequent attachment to pleasures and pleasant things—the *Rāga*; (iv) aversion to pain and unpleasant things—the *Dveṣa*; and (v) desire for life or the love of it—'the will to be'—called the *Abhiniveśa*.

The general name for the various psychical states in the Yoga is 'citta'—literally, 'consciousness,' and yoga is really the controlling or curbing of the various processes of consciousness—*cittavṛittīnāṁ nirodhaḥ*. These processes are of a mixed nature and tend sometimes towards 'good,' that is, towards liberation, and sometimes towards 'evil,' that is, towards bondage (*saṁsāra*). The aim of the yogin is to direct them towards 'good' exclusively, by practising systematic meditation, which is yoga.

25. The Preliminaries of Yoga and The Process of Meditation.

Every yogin needs a preliminary preparation in order to be able to practise yoga. This consists of the observance of the five *yamas* and the five *niyamas*, which are the special regulations governing the life of a yogin. The *yamas* are: (a) *Ahiṁsā*—absolute harmlessness in relation to all living beings; (b) *Satya*—absolute truthfulness; (c) *Asteya*—non-stealing or honesty; (d) *Brahmacarya*—sexual restraint; and (e) *Aparigraha*—refusal to accept gifts. The five *niyamas* consist of (a) *Tapas*—assiduous application to religious life or asceticism; (b) *Svādhyāya*—a regular study of the scriptures; (c) *Īśvara-praṇidhāna*—communion with God; (d) *Śauca*—purity, both internal and external; and (e) *Santoṣa*—contentment; the last two being generally mentioned first in order. These yamas and niyamas are to be supplemented, however, by certain other moral disciplines, which really fall under harmlessness (*ahiṁsā*), and are the positive aspects of the same virtue. These are (i) *Pratipakṣa-bhāvanā*—that is trying to counteract a bad thought by conceiving a good one in its place; (ii) *Maitrī*—a spirit of friendliness towards all beings; (iii) *Karuṇā*—sympathy; (iv) *Muditā*—cheerfulness with a view to making others happy; and (v) *Upekṣā* (literally, 'indifference')—toleration. When the mind, or rather the mentality of the yogin is purified by practising these virtues, he can proceed to apply himself to meditation which should be carried on without interruption (*abhyāsa*); with faith (*śraddhā*); with strength of purpose (*vīrya*); and with wisdom (*prajñā*). Next follow the various processes and the stages in the practice of this meditation.

The Process of Meditation.—The actual practice of yoga consists of sitting in a steady posture (*āsana*), controlling the breath (*prāṇāyāma*) and concentrating the mind on some particular object. Any object may be chosen by the yogin for concentration, although it is recommended that it should be God. Repeated efforts to keep the mind fixed upon the object of concentration is called 'dhyāna.' This practice brings about a state of mind in which the distinction of the subject and the object is lost, and the mind becomes one with the object of its attention, and is completely fixed. This stage is that of *samādhi*, which itself admits of six successive steps. These are: (i) The *Savitarka* stage, in which the name and the qualities of the object of concentration are present to the mind; (ii) The *Nirvitarka*, that in which the name and the qualities are absent from consciousness; (iii) The *Savicāra*—the one in which the mind concentrates upon the five 'subtle elements' (the *tanmātrās*) with a congnizance of their qualities; (iv) The *Nirvicāra*—when the mind is one with these subtle elements without any consciousness of their qualities; (*v*) *Ānanda*—that which is characterised by a concentration of the mind upon the activity of the intellect in relation to the object of attention; (vi) *Asmitā*—the concentration of the intellect on pure substance as divested of all distinctions. All these stages, however, constitute what has been called the *Samprajñāta Samādhi*, that is, one in which the mind concentrates upon some object and is conscious of its existence as such. The last stage of concentration is known as the *Asamprajñāta* or *Nirodha Samādhi*, in which the mind becomes completely identified with the object, and is therefore without any object. This state, when retained by the yogin for a long time, brings about a destruction of all the old potencies (*saṁskāras*), which are the cause of fresh action and, therefore, of birth and death. These being destroyed, the intellect becomes pure and then dawns true knowledge, which leads to liberation. This enlightenment consists chiefly of a consciousness of the fact that the world is a source of suffering and misery, and that the true self is pure and different from matter, attachment to which is the cause of bondage. It must be noted that liberation or salvation, according to the Sāṁkhya and the Yoga doctrine, is devoid of bliss or happiness, for all feeling belongs to *prakṛiti*. It is a state of pure intelligence.

26. The Development of the Yoga Literature.

It has to be admitted that a mention of the methods of concentration is found as early as the Kṛiṣṇa Yajurveda. However, it is in the Maitrāyaṇīya Upaniṣad that we find traces of a systematic development of the Yoga. The other two earlier Upaniṣads, which mention it, are the Śvetāśvatara and the Kaṭha. It is instructive to note that it is in the same Upaniṣads that we find clear traces of the Sāṁkhya metaphysics. The Upaniṣads which predominantly identify themselves with the Yoga doctrine are Śāṇḍīlya, Yogatattva, Dhyānabindu, Haṁsa, Amritanāda, Varāha, Yogakuṇḍalī, and Nādabindu. An examination of these Upaniṣads shows that the Yoga practices underwent several changes in the course of time, and particular kinds of practices were associated with particular schools. The Śaiva and the Śākta schools developed a peculiar form known as the Mantrayoga. Another form was the Haṭhayoga, which was supposed to confer upon the yogin supernatural powers and consisted of a number of elaborate nervous exercises.

However, it is in the Yoga Sūtras of Patañjali that we first find a scientific exposition of the Yoga doctrine. In them the author has tried to co-ordinate the different forms of Yoga practices which admitted of co-ordination, and has grafted the Yoga doctrine on the Sāṁkhya metaphysics. The date of the Yoga Sūtras could not be earlier than the Second Century B.C.

The Yoga Sūtras were followed by a number of standard commentaries, which by themselves are of some value. The first commentary was the Vyāsabhāṣya by Vyāsa (about 400 A.D.). The Vyāsabhāṣya itself was commented on by Vācaspati Miśra, Vijñāna Bhikṣu, Bhoja and Nāgeśa. Their commentaries are known as Tattva Vaiśāridī, Yogavārtika, Bhojavṛitti and Chāyāvyākhyā respectively.

There has been a difference of opinion with regard to the date of Patañjali—the author of the Yoga Sūtras, the chief point of controversy being the possibility of his being identified with the author of the Mahābhāṣya, the great commentary on Paṇini's grammar. The great Indian commentators, and following them several Western scholars, consider the author of the two works to be the same person—Patañjali. Prof. J. H. Woods of Harvard University is one of those who are not willing to accept this identity of authorship. A close examination of the Mahābhāṣya, however, as has been pointed out by Professor S. N. Das Gupta in his History of Indian Philosophy, does not reveal anything which may be regarded as a proof of the non-identity of the two Patañjalis. On the other hand, there are certain similarities, for example, the way in which the two works begin, which may well suggest that both can be attributed to one and the same author. Taking this into consineration as well as the fact that the first three chapters of the Yoga Sūtras, which seem to have originally constituted the entire work, are free from polemical references to the later aspects of Buddhism, one is inclined to place the date of the Yoga Sūtras somewhere near the Second Century before Christ.

Before closing this section on the Yoga Philosophy mention must be made of another work—Kitāb Pātañjala—of which Alberuni speaks, and attention to which has been drawn by Professor S. N. Das Gupta in his History of Indian Philosophy. This was written in the form of a dialogue, and although called the Book of Patañjali, it must have been different from the Yoga Sūtras of Patañjali. It also was intended to be a work on Yoga Philosophy, but the doctrines it represents are conspicuously different from those contained in the Yoga Sūtras and reveal a modification of the Yoga System so as to bring it more into line with the Vedāntic trend of thought. Professor Das Gupta has given an excellent summary of the divergent points in the new system, and we quote it here for the sake of our readers. He writes: "The difference of this system from that of the Yoga Sūtras is: (i) the conception of God has risen to such importance that He has become the only object of meditation, and absorption in Him is the goal; (ii) the importance of the *Yama* and the *Niyama* has been reduced to the minimum; (iii) the value of the Yoga discipline as a separate means of salvation apart from any connection with God, as we find it in the Yoga Sūtras, has been lost sight of; (iv) liberation and Yoga are defined as absorption in God; (v) the introduction of Brahman; (vi) the very significance of Yoga as control of mental states is lost sight of and (vii) Alchemy (*rasāyana*) is introduced as one of the means of salvation." The date of this work has been assigned to somewhere near the Third or the Fourth Century of the Christian era.

It may be noted that the earlier Yoga Philosophy presents remarkable resemblance to Jainism and Buddhism in the nature of the Yoga discipline and its consistently predominant note of pessimism. The scope and the ideal of Yoga are the same as the four sacred truths of the Buddhists (the *āryasatyāni*), namely, the existence of suffering, the origin of suffering, the possibility of the removal of suffering, and the means of the removal of suffering.

THE MĪMĀṀSĀ SYSTEM OR THE PŪRVA MĪMĀṀSĀ

27. The Essentials of the Pūrva Mīmāṁsā.

The chief work of this system is the Mīmāṁsā Sūtras of Jaimini, also known as the Pūrva Mīmāṁsā as distinguished from the Uttara Mīmāṁsā of Bādarāyaṇa called the Vedānta Sūtras. Strictly speaking, this doctrine represents a sacrificial system which has its origin in the Brāhmaṇas. As the observance of the various kinds of sacrifices became widespread, in the course of time, there naturally grew up a body of rules and regulations relating to these rites and ceremonies. These became complex and at times divergent in different circles of priests, and a satisfactory systematisation and co-ordination of them were needed. Such an attempt was made by Jaimini in his Mīmāṁsā Sūtrasṁ, which may be taken as a body of the rules and regulations calculated to guide one in the interpretation of the Vedic texts as applied to sacrificial rites. And as far as this subject of the Mīmāṁsa doctrine is concerned, it has little interest from the point of view of pure philosophy. However, as a complete system, this school of thought too has its own views with regard to the existence and the nature of God, matter and soul, and has in addition a few other peculiarities, which we shall presently notice.

The Mīmāṁsā Metaphysics.—In the Mīmāṁsā Metaphysics there is no place for God. The world and the word are regarded as eternal, and hence they do not require any creator. The universe goes on, as it is, mechanically for ever. The Vedas are also eternal and do not depend for their authority on any such being as

God. The individual souls exist and are real, and it is for them that the Vedic texts prescribe sacrifices as the means of attaining to heaven. The soul is distinct from the body and it is eternal. It is manifested to us in all cognitions and in introspection. Matter is also real and eternal. Salvation consists of the freedom of souls from the bondage of birth and death. It is achieved by exhausting the fruits of past actions and stopping all further activity which has any beneficent results for its purpose.

The Self-validity of Knowledge and the Theory of Illusion.—The most important doctrine of the Mīmāṁsā Philosophy is the self-validity of knowledge (*svataḥ-prāmāṇya*), as distinguished from the opposite theory of the Nyāya System (*parataḥ-prāmāṇya*), according to which mere perception is no proof of the validity of knowledge. The doctrine of the self-validity of knowledge in the Mīmāṁsā maintains that all knowledge, except that due to memory, is valid in itself and requires no other proof for the certitude of its truth.

This doctrine naturally raises the problem of the nature of illusions. If all knowledge due to perception is valid in itself, what explanation is there of the possibility of illusions? The subject of illusion has been discussed by almost all the systems of Indian Philosophy, and leaving out the metaphysical theory of illusion in the Vedānta—that of the *Māyā*—the psychological doctrine appears under particular names with the different schools of thought. They are: (1) The *Satkhyāti* of the Jainas; (2) The *Ātmakhyāti* of the Buddhists; (3) The *Viparīta-khyāti* or the *Anyathākhyāti* of the Nyāya, the Vaiśeṣika and the Yoga; and (4) The *Akhyāti* of the Mīmāṁsā school. The two most common examples of illusion in Indian Philosophy are those of a rope appearing to be a snake in darkness, and that of a piece of conch-shell perceived as silver. Now the *Satkhyāti* doctrine of the Jainas says that illusion consists of perceiving a thing in wrong spatial and temporal relations. The snake does exist, but not in that particular place and at that particular time where and when the rope actually exists. So the illusion is a 'mis-relationing of existents.' The *Ātmakhyāti* of the Buddhists regards illusion as exclusively subjective. According to Buddhistic idealism there is no external world. The whole of reality and the knowledge of it consists of a flow of ideas, which creates both the perceiver and the perceived, and also unites them. Correct perception and illusion are both forms of this internal knowledge, independently of any external data, for there are no such in existence. The Nyāya, the Vaiśeṣika and the Yoga are realistic schools of thought, and consequently they object to this Buddhistic explanation of illusion, and account for it by what is known as the *Viparītakhyāti* or the *Anyathākhyāti* theory. It holds that illusion is due to mal-observation in which the peculiar qualities of the object which actually exists, and of that which is wrongly perceived, are not noticed. A certain feature, or features, common to both is noticed; for example, the glow common to a piece of silver and a conch-shell; and by the accidental remembrance of a piece of silver seen in the past, the present object of perception is also taken to be a piece of the same metal. This fact of remembering a piece of silver, however, is not taken note of at the time of the illusion. The theory holds that in addition to a failure to distinguish between the object which actually exists and that which is wrongly perceived, in every illusion there is also a positive false identification of the one with the other; for example, of a piece of silver with a piece of conch-shell. The *Akhyāti* theory of the Mīmāṁsā School does not recognise this last positive element. It says that as the peculiar features of the piece of conch-shell are not perceived at all, it is wrong to say that it is identified with a piece of silver. Although illusion is partly remembrance and partly apprehension, owing to the fact that this act of remembrance is not consciously taken note of at the time of false apprehension, the illusory perception also appears to be as true and valid as a correct perception. Thus knowledge arising out of illusion is for the time being as self-evident and self-valid as that due to correct perception. This illusory knowledge can, however, be rejected or corrected in the light of subsequent experience. The chief point to be remembered about this theory of illusion is that it is not due to any positive wrong knowledge, but simply to the negative factor of the non-apprehension of certain differences in the act of perception.

It may be pointed out that the Mīmāṁsā School emphasised this doctrine of the self-validity of knowledge and of the eternal nature of the word in order to secure an independent validity and eternity for the Vedas, which form the supreme authority in this system. As already indicated, the main subject of this philosophy is a classification of the Vedic injunctions and an enunciation of the main principles of interpreting the Vedic texts. A detailed explanation of these is out of place in such a treatise as this, which is intended to be as brief and as close to pure philosophy as possible.

28. The Mīmāṁsā Literature.

As already stated the chief work of the System is Jaimini's Mīmāṁsa Sūtras. Almost all the later works are either commentaries or sub-commentaries upon it.

Some minor works are merely expositions of the doctrines represented by the Sūtras and their commentaries. The Mīmāṁsā Sūtras were written about 200 B.C. The chief and the most universally recognised commentary on these is that of Śabara Svāmin known as the Śabarabhāṣya, and this forms the basis of all subsequent Mīmāṁsā literature. The two other conspicuous persons who wrote commentaries on the Śabarabhāṣya were Kumārila and his pupil Prabhākara. Kumārila's work is divided into three parts known as (1) Ślokavārtika, (2) Tantravārtika, and (3) Tuptīkā. Prabhākara's commentary is called Bṛihatī, and is believed to have been based upon the work of another person who is referred to by him as Vārtikakāra. Prabhākara's Bṛihatī was in its turn commented upon by Śālikanātha Miśra, whose work is known as Ṛijuvimalā. Next to Kumārila and Prabhākara comes the great Mīmāṁsā scholar Maṇḍana Miśra—the author of Vidhiviveka, Mīmāṁsānukramiṇī and a commentary of Tantravārtika. This follower of Kumārila was converted to Vedāntism by Śaṁkarācārya later on. The date of Śabara Svāmin is placed approximately somewhere near 57 B.C. by Dr. Gaṅgānātha Jhā, while it is recognised that Kumārila was the senior contemporary of the great Vedāntist Śaṁkarācārya. Among a large number of other followers of Kumārila the names of Sucarita Miśra, Someśvara, Rāmakṛiṣṇa Bhatta, Somanātha, Mādhava, Śaṁkara Bhatta, Vācaspati Miśra, Anantadeva and Gāgabhatta are worthy of notice. None of these made any fresh advance beyond Śabara Svāmin, Kumārila and Prabhākara, and in fact the whole of Mīmāṁsā literature is only an exposition and elaboration of the views of these three great luminaries of the ritualistic philosophy.

THE UTTARA MĪMĀṀSĀ OR THE VEDĀNTA

29. General Introduction.

We have seen that the system of philosophy, which deals with ritualism, is known as the Pūrva Mīmāṁsā or simply the Mīmāṁsā. Now, the school of thought, which lays emphasis upon what is technically known as the 'Path of Knowledge' (*Jñānamārga*), is called the Uttara Mīmāṁsā or the Vedānta. The Pūrva Mīmāṁsā is so called because it is based upon the Brāhmaṇas, which are recognised as the earlier part of the Vedic literature, and the name means 'a discourse dealing with the earlier part.' The Uttara Mīmāṁsā or the Vedānta owes its origin to the Upaniṣads, which are considered to be the latter or the last part of the Vedas, and hence the appellation, which signifies 'a review of the latter or the last part.' While the Pūrva Mīmāṁsā discusses the ritualistic aspect of the teachings of the Vedas and the Brāhmaṇas, the Vedānta develops and systematises the philosophical implications of the texts of the various Upaniṣads. Thus, all Vedānta, of whatever form it may be, is essentially speculative in its character, and sometimes provides a scathing criticism of the ritualistic doctrine upheld by the other school. Further, as a school of thought it usually stands for monism, that is, for the doctrine that the ultimate reality is one and one only—that of Brahman (the universal self). This doctrine of monism, however, assumes a number of specific forms in the history of philosophy, and therefore, in order to trace the origin and development of the Vedānta, we shall have to see how it has its beginnings in the Vedas and the Upaniṣads (*Śruti*) and how it has developed subsequently in the hands of such individual teachers as Gauḍapāda, Śaṁkarācārya, Rāmānujācārya, Vallabhācārya and their followers. The most illustrious and by far the most influential of these was the great Śaṁkarācārya, and his doctrines enjoyed so widespread a reputation that usually the philosophy of the Vedānta is understood to be identical with his own peculiar doctrines. It will be seen presently, however, that he represents only one particular school of the monistic thought of India. But first of all we must try to see how the foundations of the whole Vedāntic system are laid deep in the verses of the earliest of the Vedas and in the texts of the Upaniṣads.

30. Vedānta in the Vedas and the Upaniṣads.

The germs of the Vedāntic doctrine of the unity of existence may be found as early as the Ṛigveda, which is the earliest of all the Vedas. The text: *ekaṁ sad vipra bahudha vadanti*—'the poets give many names to that which is only one' (Ṛig., I. 164. 46)—indicates, in as clear terms as possible, that plurality is a mere matter of words, and that unity alone is real. Similar is the implication of the text: "This entire universe is the *puruṣa* alone, both that which was and that which endures for the future"—(Ṛig., X. 90. 2). And there is quite a large number of texts from the Vedas which can be quoted to show that monism was not an unfamiliar doctrine to the Vedic sages.

However, the real beginnings of the systematic Vedānta Philosophy are supposed to be found in the teachings of the Upaniṣads, although it has to be remembered that all the Upaniṣads are not necessarily monistic in thought. It is only a few important ones of these that stand for an unqualified pure monism. The Upaniṣads were considered to be a part of *Śruti*—the revealed literature, and hence the texts of these were supposed to have an unquestionable divine authority. Consequently, the individual thinkers, who, almost all, were anxious to be loyal to the revealed texts, entered on the arduous labour of interpreting the important texts with a view to finding in them a support for their own philosophy.

Some of the texts of the Upaniṣads, known as the *Mahāvākyas*—'the great texts'—are expressive of the monistic doctrine in as clear and brief a form as possible. They are such as: *Tattvamasi*—'That thou art'; *Ekamevādvitīyam*—'Only one without a second'; *Etadātmyaṁ idaṁ sarvam*—'All this has this for its self'; *Sarvaṁ khalu idaṁ Brahma*—'All this is verily Brahman'; *Ahaṁ brahmāsmi*—'I am Brahman.' Others are ambiguous, and an effort is made by both the dualists and the monists to interpret them in their own way. The Vedānta Sūtras of Bādarāyaṇa, which form the chief systematic treatise of the Vedānta, have been found to refer to the texts of the Chāndogya, the Bṛihadāraṇyaka, the Kaṭhaka, the Taittirīya, Kauṣītaki, the Muṇḍaka and the Praśna Upaniṣads. And all these may be taken as predominantly monistic in their teachings. A few quotations from these bearing upon the subject are given here to show the nature of their thought:

(i) *Etad eva somya idam agra āsīt, ekam eva advitīyam.*—'Being only this was in the beginning, one without a second.' —Chānd., VI. 2. 1.

(ii) *Ātmā vā idam eka eva agra āsīt*—'In the beginning all this was self—one only.'—Ait. Ar., II. 4.

(iii) *Ayam ātmā Brahma sarvānubhūḥ*—'This self is Brahman perceiving everything.'—Bṛih., II. 5. 19.

That Brahman is the source of all the diverse aspects of reality is the pervading note of most of the Upaniṣads. The following quotations will be found interesting :—

> "Fire is his head, his eyes sun and moon,
> His ears the regions of the sky,
> The revealed Veda is his voice,
> The wind his breath, the universe his heart, from his feet is the earth,
> He is the inmost self in all things."—Muṇḍ., 2. 1. 4.

> "As a spider ejects and retracts (the threads),
> As the plants shoot forth on the earth,
> As the hairs on the head and body of the living man,
> Go from the unperishable all that is here.
> As the sparks from the well-kindled fire,
> In nature akin to it, spring forth in their thousands ;
> So, my dear sir, from the imperishable
> Living beings of many kinds go forth,
> And again return into him."—Bṛih., 2. 1. 20.

The following quotation from Kaṭha Upaniṣad denies plurality in the clearest possible terms :—

> (1) "That which is here is also there,
> Thatwhich is there is also here.
> From death to new death he rushes,
> Who fancies that he here sees difference !"

(2) " In the spirit should this be noted,
Here there is no plurality at all,
From death to new death he strides,
Who fancies that he here sees difference."[1]

Besides being considered the only form of ultimate reality, in these Upaniṣads Brahman is described as one that transcends all relations of substance and attribute, cause and effect, and time and space. It is the cosmic principle. It is also beyond the moral distinctions of good and evil. And in spite of all that is said about the nature of this ultimate principle, it is considered unknowable—something beyond the reach of reason. Any number of quotations can be given from the Upaniṣads which embody this doctrine of Brahman. In the Bṛihadāraṇyaka Upaniṣad we find Yājñavalkya describing Brahman thus: "He, however, the *ātman*, is not so, not so (*neti neti*). He is incomprehensible, for he is not comprehended, indestructible, for he is not destroyed; unaffected, for nothing affects him; he is not fettered, he is not disturbed, he suffers no harm!"

Thus the Vedānta, so far as it emphasizes the unity of existence, is evidently present in most of the Upaniṣads. The doctrine of *Māyā*, that is the view that the world of experience is an illusion, which, as we shall see, forms the peculiar feature of Śaṃkara's Vedānta, is not discernible until as late as the Śvetāśvatara Upaniṣad, although it may be taken as implied in the absolute undifferentiated principle of ultimate reality, which forms the essential teaching of most of the Upaniṣads.

In the sequel we shall have occasion to discuss certain other texts of the Upaniṣads when we consider the doctrine as it is held by the later individual thinkers.

---

[1] The translation into English verse is adopted from Paul Deussen's 'The Philosophy of the Upaniṣads.'

31. The Vedānta of Gauḍapāda.

Gauḍapāda was the first systematic expounder of the monistic doctrine which came to be known as the Vedānta. In his work Māṇḍūkyakārikā he does not refer to any previous teacher of Vedānta, and Śaṁkara in his commentary upon this Kārikā gives the credit for formulating and systematising the doctrine of unity to Gauḍapāda and not to Bādarāyaṇa—the author of the Vedānta Sūtras. The reason probably is, that, during the time of Śaṁkara, and even previously to him, the Vedānta Sūtras were not considered to represent a purely monistic philosophy. Later on, too, we know that the Vaiṣṇava commentators of the work have reaḍ a modified dualism in this work.

Gauḍapāda was the teacher of Govinda, and the latter was the teacher of Śaṁkara. It is quite probable that Śaṁkara was a student in the latter part of Gauḍapāda's life. Śaṁkara, in fact, acknowledges that he was directly influenced by the teachings of Gauḍapāda. Thus Gauḍapāda must have lived somewhere near the VIIIth Century A.D.

An examination of Gauḍapāda's Kārikā shows that Gauḍapāda, if not a confirmed Buddhist, was very much impressed by the teachings of Buddha and considered that these were not necessarily opposed to the monistic philosophy of the Upaniṣads.

Gauḍapāda's Māṇḍūkyakārikā is divided into four chapters. In the first chapter he explains the three apparent manifestations of the self—*viz.*, (*a*) as the *Vaiśvānara ātmā*—the self as conscious of the world in the state of waking; (*b*) as the *taijasa ātmā*—the self as conscious in the state of dream; and (*c*) *Suṣupti ātmā*—the self as it is in the state of deep sleep when there is no determinate knowledge and the self stands in its own pure consciousness and pure bliss. However, these states do not reveal the true nature of the self, and Gauḍapāda says that the fourth state of the *ātman* is that in which it is beyond perception, relation, comprehension, definition or expression, has for its essence unity of the self, is characterised by the extinction of phenomenal reality, is quiescent, the good and the one. In Saṁskṛit terminology, it is *adṛiṣta, avyavahāryam, agrāhyam, alakṣaṇa, acintyam, avyapadeśyam, ekātmapratyayasāra, prapañcopaśama, śāntam, śivam* and *advaita.* This represents the real nature of the self. In the second chapter, Gauḍapāda explains how the world of experience is unreal. He attributes the perception of all phenomena to illusion. In fact, there is no relation of cause and effect; nor is there any bondage or liberation. The third chapter elaborates the same idea of illusory appearance due to *māyā.* The fourth chapter is devoted mainly to the discussion of the relation of cause and effect, and it is pointed out by means of a dialectical form of argument that there is only the appearance of change and production in things, and that the ultimate reality is unproduced, unchangeable, non-substantial and completely unmoved. "That things exist, do not exist; that they are moving or steady; or none of those; are but thoughts with which fools are deluded." Such is the philosophy of Gauḍapāda, and it should be quite easy to see that there is practically no difference between what he said and what Śaṁkara elaborated later on with regard to the nature of the phenomenal world of experience and the noumenal world of reality.

32. The Vedānta of Śaṁkarācarya.

Śaṁkarācārya was born about 750 A. D. in the Malabar country (South India—Deccan). His father's name was

Śivaguru, who was a Yajurvedi Brāhmaṇa of the Taittirīya Branch. Śaṁkara is believed to be an incarnation of the god Śiva and is reported to have performed a number of miracles. It is said he was the pupil of Govinda, who was a student of Gauḍapāda. There is reason to believe that Śaṁkara came into contact with Gauḍapāda also, and was thus influenced by his philosophy. From such biographies of Śaṁkara as are available in Saṁskṛit, *e.g.*, Śaṁkara-digvijaya, Śaṁkara-vijaya-vilāsa and Śaṁkara-jaya, it appears that he finished his education at a very early age and entered upon an extensive tour of propaganda against Buddhism and the Mīmāṁsā school. He held discourses and discussions with learned pandits and sages wherever he went and established his own doctrines by conquering them. One of these remarkable conquests in dialectics was that of the great Mīmāṁsā teacher Maṇḍana Miśra, who was converted to his views and became an ascetic follower of his own. According to tradition Śaṁkara died at the early age of thirty-two, although there is reason to believe that he must have lived much longer.

Before we undertake an exposition of the Vedānta of Śaṁkarācārya and the other Ācāryas it is important to point out that neither Śaṁkara nor any of his successors ever claimed to have formulated an original system of philosophy. As already mentioned, the chief systematic work of the Vedānta school of thought is the Vedānta Sūtras of Bādarāyaṇa, which is intended to embody the teachings of the Upaniṣads in an abridged form. The aphorisms are so terse and admit of so varied an interpretation that it is very difficult to say exactly what particular line of thought they in themselves represent. Like every other aphoristic treatise they have always been studied with the help of some commentary or other, which must have been the result of traditional instruction in the subject. There is internal evidence in the commentaries of Śaṁkara and Rāmānuja, which goes to show that there were commentators on the Vedānta Sūtras even before Śaṁkara. The name of Baudhāyana is definitely mentioned as one of the commentators by Rāmānuja. Draviḍācārya was another Vedāntic commentator. The date of Bādarāyaṇa cannot be ascertained exactly. Taking into consideration the whole of the circumstantial evidence all that we can say is that he must have lived before Pāṇini—the famous grammarian and earlier than the period of the Bhagavadgītā.

The earliest commentary on the Vedānta Sūtras available to us is that of Śaṁkarācārya, which, according to tradition, he wrote when he was only twelve. It is in his commentary of the Sūtras and in that of a number of Upaniṣads and the Bhagavadgītā that we find an exposition of his philosophy. The commentary on the Sūtras aims at showing that the references in the Sūtras are to such texts of the Upaniṣads as embody the monistic teaching. Besides, there is a good deal of dialectical argument to prove that the doctrines of the dualistic and the atheistic schools are false. In spite of Śaṁkara's ability to employ sometimes extremely subtle argumentation, with him logical reasoning has only a very secondary value and is not to be trusted for the solution of the problem of ultimate truth. Divine Revelation or 'Śruti' is the only reliable guide, and reasoning is to be employed only to support what is revealed and not to contradict it.

Without going into the details of the controversy we give here in outline the main points of Śaṁkara's philosophy. The keynote to the whole philosophy of Śaṁkara is to be found in the opening lines of his commentary on the Vedānta Sūtras, which, as translated into English by Dr. Thibaut, are as follows:—

"It is a matter not requiring any proof that the object and the subject, whose respective spheres are the notion of the 'Thou' (the non-ego) and the 'Ego,' and which are opposed to each other as much as darkness and light are, cannot be identified. All the less can their respective attributes be identified. Hence it follows that it is wrong to super-impose upon the subject—whose self is intelligence, and which has for its sphere the notion of the Ego—the object whose sphere is the notion of the Non-Ego, and the attributes of the object, and *vice versa* to super-impose the subject and the attributes of the subject on the object. In spite of this it is on the part of man a natural procedure—which has its cause in wrong knowledge—not to distinguish the two entities (object and subject) and their respective attributes, although they are absolutely distinct, but to super-impose upon each the characteristic nature and the attributes of the other, and thus, coupling the real and the unreal to make use of expressions such as 'That am I,' 'That is mine.'"

On the basis of the revealed authority, as 'Śaṁkara understood it, he starts in his philosophy with the assumption that Brahman or the self is the only reality. The problem with him is to explain the world of experience—*the vyāvahārika jagat* as distinguished from the transcendent world of reality—*the pāramārthika jagat.* If Brahman is the only reality, and it is absolute, unchanged and unmoved—in fact, attributeless—what explanation is there of this world which is manifold, changing and a play of the most active forces of nature? The solution for this question Śaṁkara found in the existence of what he called '*māyā*' or '*ajñāna*'—False Knowledge, which is the cause of the illusion responsible for the appearance of the world of plurality and change. This False Knowledge is inexplicable although positive in its nature. It envelops the true reality of Brahman and makes it look unlike itself just as darkness makes a rope look like a snake. It is removable by true enlightenment which comes by leading a regulated life of renunciation and listening to the monistic teachings of a true preceptor. Salvation is the result of this spiritual enlightenment, and consists of a complete merging of the individual self in the universal self of Brahman.

To sum up, according to Śaṁkara:

(*i*) Brahman is the only reality—and it is absolute, homogeneous, impersonal and transcendent. It is the universal and the only self.

(*ii*) All differences and plurality characteristic of the world of experience are illusory, and are due to the existence of False Knowledge.

(*iii*) This False Knowledge or *māyā* is positive (*bhāvarūpa*) but inexplicable (*anirvacanīya*). It covers true reality like darkness, and is the cause of all the current distinctions of subject and object, cause and effect, good and evil, birth and death, etc. It is removable by the attainment of true knowledge.

Corresponding to the two kinds of worlds there are: (*a*) two kinds of Brahman—the true Brahman, as one absolute and transcendent; and the false or the modified Brahman, asthe 'Īśvara'—God, who is the creator, the sustainer and the destroyer of the universe; (*b*) two kinds of knowledge—the higher knowledge which reveals the true reality of Brahman, and the lower knowledge which pertains to the illusory world of experience; (*c*) two paths or modes of life—the path of true knowledge (*jñānamārga*), and that of ritualism (*karmamārga*). The former leads to salvation and the latter to a cycle of births and deaths.

(*iv*) Self-realisation or salvation is attained by acquiring true enlightenment and it consists of a complete identification of the individual self with the universal self of Brahman. It is a state in which all distinctions—even that of subject and object—disappear, and consequently a bare identity or unity of Brahman is all that is left.

It is not possible here to enter into a detailed criticism of Śaṁkara's views. However, his whole philosophy is so stimulative of thought that one cannot help pausing for a while and considering how far his propositions about the nature of reality, illusion and salvation can be borne out by reason; although it is true that with him reason and reasoning are no reliable guides or judges.

To begin with, an attributeless transcendent reality, such as Brahman is in Śaṁkara's philosophy, can form the object of neither perception nor inference, nor even intuition, and is therefore inevitably relegated to the category of the unknown and the unknowable. It is nothing more than a convenient dogmatic assumption.

Next, False Knowledge or *māyā* is a very ambiguous and vague term in Śaṁkara's system. It is said to be inexplicable and yet positive. It envelops the true reality of Brahman and is removable by the attainment of true knowledge. Now, is this *māyā* merely a subjective ignorance, or has it an objective reality ? Then, has it a beginning, or is it without a beginning ? If it has an origin, what is the cause of it ? If it has no origin, it must be co-existent with Brahman. Now these questions and issues present real difficulty to a rational thinker.

If False Knowledge is subjective ignorance, it should disappear as soon as one is told that all reality is Brahman only and the world of experience an illusion. But we find that in spite of every effort that one may make to be convinced of the truth of the Vedāntic doctrine, the world of plurality and difference stares one in the face. If it is objective, how is it going to be removed by enlightenment, which is necessarily a subjective intellectual awakening? Further, if it is a positive and objective existence, the doctrine lands itself automatically in an undeniable dualism. Similar is the difficulty of explaining the origin of False Knowledge. The cause of it cannot be found in Brahman, nor in the individual selves; for it is as different in nature from the self as darkness is from light. If it has no beginning, a monistic philosophy, such as has been propounded by Śaṁkara, is doomed.

Further, the Vedāntic salvation itself, which is the result of a sense of the complete identification of the individual and the universal self, is anything but possible consistently with Śaṁkara's theory of a transcendent Brahman. For, according to his view, Brahman is unknown and unknowable before self-realisation, and after it, the distinction of the subject and the object having disappeared, the very possibility of that *sense* of identification is taken away which forms the condition of salvation. We shall see presently, that the system of Rāmānuja, which represents a modified form of monism, is more consistent and rational. It is also true, as most of the critics of Śaṁkara have pointed out, that his peculiar monism does not really find support in the Sūtras of Bādarāyaṇa, and that Rāmānuja's interpretation of them is closer to the original doctrine of these. However, it is not possible here to go into the details of this scholastic controversy over the interpretation of the Sūtras and the texts of the Upaniṣads connected with them. We shall forthwith pass on to the Vedānta as expounded by Rāmānujācārya.

33. The Vedānta of Rāmānujacārya.

Rāmānuja's Vedānta is known as *Viśiṣṭādvaita*—'Modified Monism.' His idea of ultimate reality is that *of a Puruṣa—a* personality in the form of Brahman, *which comprehends within itself* all plurality. In fact, Rāmānuja, in his commentary on the Vedānta Sūtras known as the Śrībhāṣya, has tried to refute Śaṁkara's doctrine of the absolute Brahman and False Knowledge at every point. Like Śaṁkara, he does not claim to have founded any new school of thought. All that he does is to write a commentary on Bādarāyaṇa's work, in keeping with a certain tradition which he attributes to a number of ancient teachers, such as Baudhāyana, Dramiḍācārya or Draviḍācārya and others. Before we show in detail how Rāmānuja differed from Śaṁkara in his views, it may be pointed out that in addition to his commentary on the Vedānta Sūtras, the former has composed a treatise of his own called the Vedārtha Saṁgraha in which he mentions a number of authorities. Baudhāyana, Taṅka, Dramiḍa, Guhadeva, Kapardin, Bhāruci are the names that are enumerated, and the work contains quotations from the writings of some of these. Rāmānuja was prominent enough in his life-time to be looked upon as the founder and the head of a new sect named after him, which has quite a large number of followers even now. The Rāmānuja sect is closely allied to that of the Bhāgavatas or the Pancarātras.

As in the case of Śaṁkara, so here too, the opening lines of Rāmānuja's commentary on the Vedānta Sūtras should form a good index to the general nature of his philosophy. He begins as follows:

"May my mind be filled with devotion towards the highest Brahman, the abode of Lakṣmī; who is luminously revealed in the Upaniṣads; who in sport produces, sustains and reabsorbs the entire universe; whose only aim is to foster the manifold classes of beings that humbly worship him.

The nectar of the teaching of Parāśara's son (Vyāsa) —which was brought up from the middle of the milk-ocean of the Upaniṣads—which restores to life the souls whose vital strength had departed owing to the heat of the fire of transmigratory existence—which was well-guarded by the teachers of old—which was obscured by the mutual conflict of manifold opinions—may intelligent men daily enjoy that as it is now presented to them in my words.

The lengthy explanation *(vṛitti)* of the Brahma Sūtras, which was composed by the Reverend Bodhāyana, has been abridged by former teachers; according to their views, the words of the Sūtras will be explained in this present work."

Without going into the details of the controversy between Śaṁkara and Rāmānuja with regard to the interpretation of the Sūtras and the texts of the Upaniṣads we give below a résumé of Rāmānuja's doctrines showing how they differ from those of Śaṁkara:

(i) While according to Śaṁkara Brahman is an absolutely homogeneous, impersonal and attributeless entity, according to Rāmānuja it is a personality which comprehends within itself all plurality and difference and is characterised by all the qualities of perfection. In his commentary, after having quoted a number of texts from Viṣṇu Purāṇa he says: "These and other texts teach that the highest Brahman is essentially free from all imperfection whatsoever, comprises within itself all auspicious qualities, and finds its pastime in originating, preserving, reabsorbing, pervading and ruling the universe; that the entire complex of intelligent and non-intelligent beings (souls and matter) in all their different states is real, and constitutes the form; *i.e.*, the body of the highest Brahman . . . . The outcome of all this is that we have to cognise Brahman as carrying plurality within itself, and the world, which is the manifestation of his power, as something real."

(ii) While according to Śaṁkara, the world of experience with all its variety is illusory and the cause of it is False Knowledge, according to Rāmānuja, as indicated in the above quotation, it is quite real and forms a manifestation of the nature and powers of Brahman. The souls are individualised not because of the *upādhi* or cover of *māyā*, but because they have actually sprung up from the universal self of Brahman. Though they are never outside Brahman, yet they enjoy a separate personal existence for ever.

(iii) There is no such thing as False Knowledge or *māyā*, which according to Śaṁkara envelops Brahman and makes it appear unlike itself. Rāmānuja enters into a long argumentation to show the absurdity of this doctrine of a fictitious illusion.

(iv) With the elimination of 'Illusion' the doctrine of a false Brahman and a false knowledge also disappear in the system of Rāmānuja.

(v) According to Rāmānuja, Salvation or Emancipation does not consist in an absolute merging of the individual soul in Brahman, but in its passing from the troubles of earthly life into a kind of eternal paradise, in which state also it continues to enjoy a separate personal existence. Discussing this topic in his commentary he says: "To maintain that the consciousness of the 'I' does not persist in the state of final release is again altogether inappropriate. It in fact amounts to the doctrine—only expressed in somewhat different words—that final release is the annihilation of the self. The 'I' is not a mere attribute of the self so that even after its destruction the essential nature of the self might persist—as it persists on the cessation of ignorance; but it constitutes the very nature of the self."

It is now generally recognised by scholars that Rāmānuja's interpretation of the Vedānta Sūtras is closer to the original doctrine of Bādarāyaṇa than that of Śaṁkarācārya.

The one point of criticism which should occur to a student of Rāmānuja's system is with regard to the conception of matter as something unconscious, although that also, along with the other aspect of reality—*viz.*, the spiritual—is supposed to be a manifestation of Brahman and to be contained in it. If the ultimate all-comprehensive reality is conscious and active, all its manifestations also must *ipso facto* be of the same nature. Śaṁkara was more consistent when he denied the existence of an inert, unconscious matter altogether.

Tradition ascribes Rāmānuja's birth to 938 Śāka Era, which is equivalent to about 1016 A.D. During the early years of his life he lived at Conjeeveram, and was a pupil of Yādavaprakāśa, who was known to be an adherent of Śaṁkara's Monism.

Rāmānuja's important works are Vedāntadīpa, Vedāntasāra, Vedārthasaṁgraha and the commentaries on the Bhāgavadgīta and the Brahma Sūtras.

34. Madhvācārya and his Philosophy.

Madhvācārya, known as Vāsudeva in the early part of his life, was born probably in the Śāka year 1119 corresponding to A.D. 1197. However, some put him as late as 1238 A.D. He was a pupil of Acyutapreksa and received his initiation under the name of *Pūrṇabodha* or *Pūrṇaprajña*. The place of his education was Udipi in Southern India.

As a teacher of philosophy and religion he rejected the monism (*advaita*) of Śaṁkarācārya and also the modified monism (*Viśiṣṭādvaita*) of Rāmānuja. His followers called themselves 'Sad-Vaiṣṇavas,' in order to distinguish themselves from the 'Śrīvaiṣṇava' followers of Rāmānujācārya. Madhva's system is really a dualistic philosophy, although it has been considered to be one of the forms of the monistic Vedānta.

In the philosophy of Madhvācārya the ultimate principles are first dichotomised into 'independent' and 'dependent,' of which the independent one is Viṣṇu, the Lord, and everything else being dependent. The independent principle, that is, Viṣṇu, is free from all imperfection and has inexhaustible excellences. In fact, it is this emphasis on the dependence of everything on the independent principle that entitles the system to the name of monism, although the pluralistic form of it is only too evident. Madhvācārya admits five real and eternal distinctions, *viz.*, those of (*a*) God (*paramātman*); and individual souls (*jīvātman*); (*b*) God and matter; (*c*) Individual souls and matter; (*d*) One soul and another soul; (*e*) One particle of matter and another.

The supreme being is known as Viṣṇu, Nārāyaṇa or Paro-Bhagavān and not as Brahman. He is endowed with all auspicious qualities. Viṣṇu is supposed to have Lakṣmī for his wife and has two sons—Brahman, the creator of the universe, and Vāyu, the saviour of all beings. Madhvācārya is considered to be one of the incarnations of Vāyu, and therefore is to be looked upon as the saviour of those who look up to him as their spiritual guide.

Salvation means release from transmigration and eternal residence in the abode of Nārāyaṇa.

Individual souls are characterised by ignorance, which, as in the other systems, is the cause of bondage, and is removable by the knowledge of God. There are eighteen means of acquiring this knowledge. The chief of these are: renunciation (*vairāgya*); peace (*śama*); devotion (*bhakti*); and prayer (*upāsanā*). Devotion or obedience to Viṣṇu is expressed in three ways: (1) Stigmatisation; (2) Imposition of names; and (3) Worship. Of these (1) Stigmatisation is the branding upon oneself of the weapons of Nārāyaṇa or Viṣṇu as a memorial of him, and as a means of attaining the end which is needful (emancipation); (2) Imposition of names is the appellation of sons and others by such names as *Keśava*, as a continual memorial of the Supreme Lord; (3) Worship is of ten kinds, *viz.*, *with the voice*: (*i*) veracity, (*ii*) usefulness, (*iii*) kindliness, (*iv*) sacred study; *with the body*: (*v*) almsgiving, (*vi*) defence, (*vii*) protection; *with the 'common sensory'*: (*viii*) mercy, (*ix*) longing, and (*x*) faith. Worship is the dedication of each of these to Nārāyaṇa.

The essential principles of the system may be seen in the following lines of the Bhagavadgītā, which have been quoted in the Sarvadarśanasaṁgraha:

"Two are these persons in the universe, the perishable and the imperishable;
The perishable is all the elements, the imperishable is the unmodified.
The other, the most excellent person, called the Supreme Spirit,
Is the undecaying Lord, who pervading sustains the three worlds.

Since transcending the perishable, I am more excellent than the imperishable (soul),
Hence I am celebrated among men and in the Veda as the best of persons (*puruṣottama*);
He who uninfatuated knows me thus the best of persons, he all-knowing worships me in every wise.
Thus this most mysterious institute is declared, blameless (Arjuna):
Knowing this a man may be wise, and may have done what he has to do, O Bhārata."

—Bhag., XV. 16—20.

The Literature of the System.—The chief works of the Madhva School are (i) Madhvācārya's Commentary on the Brahma Sūtras; (ii) Vāyustuti of Trivikrama—a disciple of Madhvācārya and (iii) Maṇimañjari and Madhvavijaya, both written by Nārāyaṇa, a son of Trivikrama. Of these the former deals with the religious history of India down to the birth of Madhvācārya, and the latter with the life of Madhva himself. An account of the system is also to be found in the Sarvadarśanasaṃgraha of Mādhava Ācārya.

35. Vallabhācārya and his Teachings.

Vallabhācārya, called Vallabha by his parents as a boy, was born about 1479 A.D. His father, Lakṣmaṇa Bhatta, was a Tailaṅga Brāhmaṇa and resided at Benares. This illustrious son of his is reported to have been born in a wilderness while his father was on his way to some place in the Southern India. He was looked upon as an incarnation of Kriṣṇa, and there is a number of legends about the supernatural conditions attending his birth and education. As he grew up and finished his education, he appears to have travelled to Vijayanagar and obtained a remarkable success in disputation at the court of Kṛiṣṇa Deva. After this victory over the Śaivas he was selected the spiritual head—Ācārya of the Vaiṣṇavas, and thus came to be known as Vallabhācārya. He undertook extensive travels, and ultimately settled down at Benares, where he wrote his commentary on the Bhāgavata Purāṇa, which work is really the chief basis of the system of Vallabhācārya.

The Teachings of Vallabhism.—The particular religion taught by Vallabhācārya is known as the *Puṣṭi-mārga*, a kind of Indian Epicureanism—the way of eating, drinking and enjoyment. It represents the worship of Bāla Kṛiṣṇa, that is, the adoration of Kṛiṣṇa as he was in his boyhood, according to the description of it in the Bhāgavata Purāṇa. It symbolises spiritual devotion under the figure of earthly love, and it may be pointed out that this cult developed, in the course of time, into a very coarse form of sensualism, and paved the way for extreme demoralisation among the followers of Vallabhācārya. The spiritual heads of Vallabhism are considered to be the representatives of Kṛiṣṇa himself, and their followers are supposed to have dedicated everything to them as such. These preceptors are called 'Mahārājās,' and usually lead a life characterised by the most sumptuous luxury. Those who are initiated into the cult have to take the following interesting vow, which, it may be pointed out, has been so interpreted as to allow to the 'gūrus' some of the most heinous licences that one can think of. The vow runs thus :

"I, who am suffering the infinite pain and torment produced by enduring for a thousand measured years separation from Kṛiṣṇa, do to the worshipped Kṛiṣṇa dedicate my body, organs of sense, life, heart and other faculties, and wife, house, family, property with my own self : I am thy slave—O Kṛiṣṇa."

According to Vallabhācārya, individual spirits are like sparks from the Supreme Spirit, and, though separate, are yet identical with it in essence. Consequently, the physical body, which is the abode of this divine soul, is to be carefully looked after and fed upon the choicest delicacies. Hence the whole system is saturated with a spirit of extreme hedonism. It need not be pointed out that Vallabhism is a popular religious cult rather than a serious system of philosophy. In fact the systems of Madhvācārya and Vallabhācārya represent what is known as the 'path of devotion,' the *Bhaktimārga*, and a consideration of philosophical problems has only a very secondary place with them.

The Literature of Vallabhism.—The Commentary on the Bhāgavata Purāṇa by Vallabhācārya called the Subodhinī and his Siddhāntarahasya form the main foundation of the system. Among the later works are Vacanāmrita, Gurusevā, and a commentary on the Siddhāntarahasya by Gokulanātha—one of the sons of Vallabhācārya; and the Puṣṭipravāha-maryādā-tīkā by Hararāi.

V. CONCLUSION

V. CONCLUSION

THE PRESENT OUTLOOK IN INDIAN PHILOSOPHY.

I have not much to say in the conclusion after what I have already observed in the Preface and the General Introduction. It may be mentioned that besides the main nine systems of Indian Philosophy, which find a place in this book, there are a few minor schools, or rather sects, which are offshoots of one system or the other. From the philosophical point of view they are of little importance, and hence they have been omitted here. The sect of Caitanya in Bengal, and those of Nānaka and Kabīr in the Northern India, represent a popular kind of philosophy, which although of an unsystematic nature, has a great hold upon the minds of a large section of the Indian people. In more recent times, Theosophy, Brāhmoism and the Ārya Samāja have been popular among the educated classes. However, none of them can claim to have originated any new lines of thought, and their importance chiefly lies in their being zealous advocates of religious and social reform in India.

For a long time now stagnation has prevailed in the realm of Indian Philosophy. There has been hardly any remarkable development after Rāmānuja, and at present, among the orthodox classes, the only aim of the study of the subject is to understand what has been said in the old works and their commentaries connected with their own particular sects or sections in the implicit belief that whatever is recorded there must necessarily be true. No one appears even to think of striking out any new lines of thought, or of calling in question what has been received as sacred tradition from the past. In a word, so far as the orthodox section is concerned, Indian Philosophy is still in its 'Medieval Age.' The other section represents those who have come into contact with Western Philosophy. Most of these have had no occasion to study Indian Philosophy and are consequently entirely cut off from the philosophical traditions of their own land. There is a small section of scholars who have studied the thought of both the East and the West, and it is on these that the renaissance of Indian Philosophy depends. What is needed before anything else is that the study of the subject should be drawn out of the backwaters of Archæology and orthodox Theology and made to run along with the pure living currents of Modern Philosophy. In fact, we have to remind ourselves that India can also make a contribution to the general philosophical development which is taking place among the civilised nations of the world, and that it is possible to do so on the basis of what it has been its privilege to receive by way of philosophy from the East and the West, without being necessarily hindered by such encumbrances of conventional theology as are liable to clog the wheels of progress. What is wanted is the creation of a new era in the annals of Indian Philosophy, and it may be hoped that it will be born, in the course of time, out of that union of the East and the West, which is being realised surely, although not as quickly as one might desire. The aim of this work will be more than fulfilled if it aids one to understand in outline what some of the important Indian systems of thought have to say on the problems which are ever so close to the human mind.

VI. APPENDICES.

VI. APPENDICES

(i)

GERMS OF MODERN PSYCHOLOGY IN THE YAJURVEDA.

(*A paper accepted for presentation to the Third Session of the Indian Philosophical Congress.*)

(An Appendix to Part I, Section 2.)

In spite of the fact that the Vedas are the oldest and, therefore, the most primitive records of human thought, and cannot, for that reason, be expected to embody advanced views on scientific and philosophical subjects, the fact remains that some portions of them contain wonderful germs of modern speculation. That is why that devoted scholar of Oriental learning—the late Professor Max Müller, said about them that 'they are to us unique and priceless guides in opening before our eyes tombs of thought richer in relics than the royal tombs of Egypt, and more ancient and primitive in thought than the oldest hymns of Babylonian or Arcadian poets.' The writer of this paper is aware of the fact that some people have tried to find in the Vedas what probably they do not contain, and such an effort is certainly unworthy of the sacred vocation of the votaries of truth. But it would be equally unworthy of their calling, if they fail to notice and bring to the notice of others such grains of scientific and philosophic truths as may actually be found lying in juxtaposition with the other kind of material which constitutes the Vedic lore. The Vedas are no systematic treatises on science or philosophy, and most of the Vedic verses are hymns to a number of gods and goddesses, who usually are personifications of the forces of nature. But it is in these very hymns that we can sometimes discover the germs of some profound doctrines of philosophy and religion. So far a good deal has been written on the metaphysical implications of these hymns, and it is true that such is their most usual and direct significance. The object of this paper is to draw the attention of scholars to the first six verses of the 34th chapter of the Yajurveda, which contain a description of mind remarkably beautiful and wonderfully modern, and which, therefore, should be of great interest to a student of Psychology. I shall quote the original verses first and give an English rendering of the same:—

> 'Yajjāgrato dūramudaiti daivaṁ tadu suptasya tathaivaiti,
> Dūraṅgamaṁ jyotiṣāṁ jyotirekaṁ tanme manaḥ śiva-
> saṁkalpamastu.'

May that mind of mine conceive noble ideas, which, endowed with divine qualities, traverses long distances, both when a person is awake and asleep; that which travels far and wide, and is the light of lights, that is, the ultimate source of all knowledge.—(1)

> 'Yena karmāṇyapaso manīṣiṇo yajñe kriṇvanti vidatheṣu
> dhīrāḥ,
> Yadapūrvaṁ yakṣamantaḥ prajānāṁ tanme manaḥ
> śivasaṁkalpamastu.'

May that mind of mine be of auspicious ideas, with the aid of which constant and wise men perform their duties pertaining to sacrifice and war; that which is a wonderful sacred thing seated in the self of all beings.—(2)

> 'Yatprajñānamuta ceto dhṛtiśca yajjyotirantaramṛitaṁ
> prajāsu,
> Yasmānn rite kiṁcana karma kriyate tanme manaḥ śiva-
> saṁkalpamastu.'

May that mind of mine cherish noble thoughts, which is (of the nature of) intelligence, emotional consciousness and resolution, and the eternal (undecaying) light in the self of all beings; that without which nothing can be accomplished.—(3)

'Yenedam bhūtaṁ bhuvanaṁ bhaviṣyat parigṛihītam-amṛitena sarvaṁ,
Yena yajñastāyete saptahotā tanme manaḥ śiva-saṁkalpamastu.'

May that mind of mine be pure, which being eternal holds the past, the present and the future all together; that with the aid of which that sacrifice is performed in which seven persons take part.—(4)

'Yasminnṛicaḥ sāmayajūṁṣi yasmin pratiṣṭhitā ratha-nābhāvivārāḥ,
Yasminścittaṁ sarvamotaṁ prajānāṁ tanme manaḥ śivasaṁkalpamastu.'

May that mind of mine think nobly, in which the Ṛig, the Sāma and the Yajur Vedas are held together like spokes in the navel of a chariot-wheel, and in which all the contents of consciousness are held together (like beads in a necklace).—(5)

'Suṣārathiraśvāniva yanmanuṣyān nenīyate bhīśubhir vājina iva,
Hṛitpratiṣṭhaṁ yadajiraṁ javiṣṭhaṁ tanme manaḥ śiva-saṁkalpamastu.'

May that mind of mine be of high thinking, which leads and controls men, just as a good charioteer does the horses by holding the reins; that which residing in the heart of men is the swiftest of all and free from decay.—(6)

—Yajurveda, XXXIV. 1—6.

The above verses mention a number of important characteristics of mind and mental life. In the first place, the fact, that mind is described as 'daivam'—divine, *and 'amṛitam'—immortal, clearly implies that* it is not regarded as a physical thing, and, therefore, it is not to be identified with the body or the brain; nor is it to be regarded as the function of the same. This conception of mind is very much allied to the conception of self in Metaphysics, and presents a contrast to the later view in Indian Philosophy, according to which, mind is only an 'indriya'—a sense-organ, like the other sense-organs. This conception of mind as something non-material is further corroborated by the fact that it is described as 'dūraṅgamam'—that which traverses long distances, and also 'javiṣṭham'—the swiftest of all; the implication being that unlike material objects, including our bodies, it is unhampered in its activity by the limitations of time and space.

The next point, and the one which is the most remarkable, about the description of mind as given in the third of the above verses, is the threefold character of the same as 'prajñāna'—intelligence or cognition, 'cetaḥ'—emotional consciousness or feeling, and 'dhṛitiḥ'—resolution or will. It does not need any particular effort of one's imagination, or a distortion of the meaning of the terms used in the verse, in order to discover this meaning, although it is true that this verse has not so far attracted the notice of scholars as one of such definite psychological significance. The words 'prajñāna' and 'cetaḥ' have been loosely translated as 'consciousness,' although the distinction in the meaning of the two words, as made in this paper, is not unusual even in the post-Vedic literature; for example, compare the use of 'cetānisi' in the following verse of the Uttaracarita:

Vajrādapi kaṭhorāṇi mṛidūni kusumādapi,
Lokottarāṇaṁ cetānisi ko nu vijñatumarhasi.

The description of mind given in the other five verses distinctly bears out the above interpretation of the third verse: In the first verse, mind is said to be the light of all lights, that is to say, the ultimate source or instrument of knowledge. The same intellectual or cognitive aspect of mental life is beautifully described in the fourth and fifth verses by calling mind the abiding and unifying principle of knowledge—'that which being eternal holds the past, the present and the future—all together'; 'that in which the Ṛig, the Sāma and the Yajur Vedas are held together like spokes in the navel of a chariot-wheel, and in which all the contents of consciousness are held together like beads in a necklace.' The sixth verse brings out the practical or volitional aspect of mind: 'that which leads and controls men just as a good charioteer does the horses by holding the reins.' Similarly in the second and the third verses: 'That with the aid of which constant and wise men perform their duties pertaining to sacrifice and war'; 'that without which nothing can be accomplished.' Then at the end of each verse there is a prayer that the mind be endowed with noble and auspicious feelings.

Thus a careful study of the above verses in the Yajurveda would show that, besides a definite recognition of the modern tripartite division of mental life, the conception of mind is so akin to that of self in Metaphysics, and therefore so modern from the psychological point of view. For, whatever may be the differences among psychologists about some of the details of mental life, it is almost a common creed with them that broadly speaking what is self to Metaphysics is mind to Psychology; that mind is not one particular faculty, but one whole psychic unity, which, so far as Psychology is concerned, is as permanent and ultimate as the 'self' of Metaphysics.

BIBLIOGRAPHY

BIBLIOGRAPHY

THE PHILOSOPHY OF THE VEDIC PERIOD

THE VEDAS.

The Ṛigveda with Sāyaṇa's Commentary: English Translation by Wilson and Griffith.

The Ṛigveda: English Translation by Kaegi.

The Yajurveda (White): English Translation by Griffith.

The Yajurveda (Black): English Translation by Keith, with Introduction and Critical Notes.

The Sāmaveda: English Translation by Rev. Stevenson.

The Atharvaveda with Sāyaṇa's Commentary: English Translations by Whitney, Griffith and Lanman.

The Vedic Hymns—Sacred Books of the East Series (S.B.E.), Vols. XXXII and XLVI—Max Müller and Oldenberg.

Original Sanskrit Texts, Vol. V—Muir.

Vedic India—Ragozin.

Six Systems of Indian Philosophy, Chapter II—Max Müller.

Lectures on the Ṛigveda—V. S. Ghate.

Vedic Mythology—Macdonell.

Vedic Reader—Macdonell.

Pre-Buddhistic Philosophy—B. Barua.

The Religion of the Veda—Bloomfield.

Indian Philosophy, Vol. I, Chap. II—Radhakrishnan.

History of Indian Philosophy, Vol. I, Chap. II—Dasgupta.

THE BRÂHMAṆAS AND THE ĀRAṆYAKAS.

The Aitareya (with Sāyaṇa's Commentary) and the Kauṣītakī Brāhmaṇas of the Ṛigveda.

The Śatapatha of the White Yajurveda and the Taittirīya of the Black Yajurveda.

The Tāṇḍya or Pañcaviṁśa and the Ṣaḍviṁśa—the chief Brāhmaṇas of the Sāmaveda.

The Gopatha of the Atharvaveda.

The Aitareya Āraṇyaka with Sāyaṇa's Commentary: English Translation—S.B.E.

The Aitareya Āraṇyaka.

Indian Philosophy, Vol. I, Chap. III—Radhakrishnan.

History of Indian Philosophy, Vol. I, Chaps. II and III—Dasgupta.

THE UPANIṢADS.

The Bṛihadāraṇyaka with Saṁkara's Commentary: English Translation—S.B.E.

The Chāndogya with Śaṁkara's Commentary: English Translation—S.B.E.

The Kauṣītakī with Śaṁkara's Commentary: English Translation—S.B.E. and by Cowell.

The Śvetāśvatara with Śaṁkara's Commentary.

The Taittirīya with Śaṁkara's Commentary: English Translation—S.B.E.

Īśa, Kena, Kaṭha, Muṇḍaka: English Translation in S.B.E.

Also Mahānārāyaṇa, Praśna, Māṇḍūkya, Atharvaśiras, Nīlarudra, Brahmavidyā, Dhyānabindu and others.

The Philosophy of the Upaniṣads—Deussen.

The Philosophy of the Upaniṣads—Gough.

Pre-Buddhistic Philosophy—B. Barua.

The Thirteen Principal Upaniṣads—Hume.

The Taittirīya Upaniṣad—Mahādeva Śāstri;

Indian Philosophy, Vol. I, Chap. IV—Radhakrishnan.

History of Indian Philosophy, Vol. I, Chap. III—Dasgupta.

A Constructive Survey of the Upaniṣadic Philosophy—R. D. Ranade.

The Encyclopædia of Religion and Ethics, The Article on the Upaniṣads—The Rev. A. S. Geden.

II

THE PHILOSOPHY OF THE EPIC PERIOD

Vālmīki's Rāmāyaṇa: English Translation by Griffith.

The Mahābhārata.

The Bhagavadgītā: Saṁkara's Commentary and English Translation by Mrs. Annie Besant and others.

The Manusmṛiti: English Translation by Bühler in S.B.E.

Epic India—C. V. Vaidya.

The Bhagavadgītā, Anugītā—Telang, S.B.E.

The Great Epic of India—Hopkins.

Essays on the Gīta—Arabindo Ghosh.

The Laws of Manu: Introduction and English Translation—Bühler, S.B.E., Vol. XXV.

Indian Philosophy, Vol. I, Chaps. VIII and IX—Radhakrishnan.

III

THE PHILOSOPHY OF THE HETERODOX SCHOOLS

Materialism.

Sarvadarśanasaṁgraha: English Translation by Cowell and Gough.

Sarvasiddhāntasārasaṁgraha: English Translation by M. Raṅgācārya.

Miscellaneous Essays—Colebrooke.

Indian Philosophy, Vol. I, Chap. V—Radhakrishnan.

JAINISM.

The following works besides those mentioned in Section 2 of this book:—

Sarvadarśanasaṁgraha, Chap. III.

Sacred Books of the East Series, Vols. XXII and XLV.

The Encyclopaedia of Religion and Ethics, Vol. VII: Articles on Jainism and the Jaina Atomic Theory by Jacobi.

Tattvārtha Sūtra—Umāsvāti, Sacred Books of the Jainas.

Dravyasaṁgraha—Nemicandra, Sacred Books of the Jainas.

Pañcāstikāyasamayasāra—Kundakumudācārya, S.B.J.

Outlines of Jainism—Jaini.

The Heart of Jainism—Mrs. Stevenson.

History and Literature of Jainism—Barodia.

Indian Philosophy, Vol. I, Chap. VI—R.K.

History of Indian Philosophy, Vol. I, Chap. VI—D.G.

BUDDHISM.

The following books besides those mentioned in Section 15 of this work:—

Buddhist Mahāyāna Texts—S.B.E., Vol. I.

The Dhammapada and Sutta Nipāta—S.B.E., Vol. X.

Buddhist Suttas—S.B.E., Vol. XI.

Saddharma Puṇḍarīka S.B.E., Vol. XXI.

The Questions of King Milinda—S.B.E., Vols. XXXV and XXXVI.

Buddhism in Translations—Warren.

Buddhism—Rhys Davids.

Buddhist India—Rhys Davids.

The Dialogues of Buddha—Rhys Davids.

Buddhism—Mrs. Rhys Davids.

Buddhist Psychology—Mrs. Rhys Davids.

Anuruddha's Compendium of Philosophy—Mrs. Rhys Davids and Aung.

Mahāyāna Buddhism—Suzuki.

The Awakening of Faith—Suzuki.

The Expositor—Mrs. Rhys Davids and Maung Tin.

The Religions of India—Hopkins.

The Creed of Buddha—Holmes.

Buddha and the Gospel of Buddhism—Coomaraswamy.

Manual of Indian Buddhism—Kern.

The Way to Nirvāṇa—Poussin.

Sarvadarśanasaṁgraha, Chap. II.

Sarvasiddhāntasaṁgraha.

Śaṁkara's Commentary on the Vedānta Sūtras.

Mādhyamika Sūtras—Nāgārjuna.

Systems of Buddhistic Thought—Yamakami Sogen.

Indian Philosophy, Vol. I, Chap. VII—R.K.

History of Indian Philosophy, Vol. I, Chap. V—D.G.

IV

THE SIX SCHOOLS OF HINDU PHILOSOPHY

The Nyāya System.

Besides the works mentioned in Section 19, the following:—

Sarvadarśanasaṁgraha, Chap. XI.

Udayana's Kusumāñjali: English Translation by Cowell.

Tarkasaṁgraha: English Translation by Athalye.

Nyāya Sūtras with Vātsyāyana Bhāṣya and Uddyotakara's Vārttika: English Translation by Gaṅgānātha Jha.

Indian Logic and Atomism—Keith.

The Positive Sciences of the Ancient Hindus—B.N. Seal.

History of Indian Logic—Vidyābhūṣaṇa.

Indian Philosophy, Vol. II, Chap. II—R.K.

Six Systems of Indian Philosophy—Max Müller.

Khaṇḍanakhaṇḍakhādya: English Translation by Gaṅgānātha Jhā (Reprint from the Indian Thought).

Nyāyāvatāra of Siddhasena Divākara: English Translation by S. C. Vidyābhūṣaṇa.

Nyāyabindu of Dharmakīrti—Edition P. Peterson, B.I., 1890.

Nyāya Philosophy: Sadholal Lectures by Gaṅgānātha Jhā (published in Indian Thought).

Tarkabhāṣā of Keśavamiśra—Edition S. M. Paranjape.

Bhāṣāpariccheda: Translation by E. Roer.

A Study on Mathurānātha's Tattvacintāmaṇirahaṣya—Saileśvar Sen.

THE VAIŚEṢIKA SYSTEM.

The Vaiśeṣika Sūtras of Kaṇāda with the Upaskāra: English Translation by Nandalal Sinha.

The Vaiśeṣika System—Faddegon.

Sarvadarśanasaṁgraha, Chap. X.

Padārthadharmasaṁgraha of Praśastapāda with the Nyāyakandalī of Śrīdhara—Gaṅgānātha Jhā.

Hindu Realism—Chatterji.

Indian Logic and Atomism—Keith.

The Vaiśeṣika Philosophy—Ui.

Indian Philosophy, Vol. II, Chap. III—R.K.

History of Indian Philosophy, Vol. I, Chap. VIII—D.G.

THE SĀṀKHYA SYSTEM.

The following works besides those mentioned in Section 23 of this book:—

Sāṁkhyapravacanabhāṣya—Garbe.

Sāṁkhya Sūtravṛitti—Garbe.

Sarvadarśanasaṁgraha, Chaps. XIV and XV.

Sāṁkhya Philosophy—S. C. Banerjee.

The Sāṁkhya Philosophy—Nandalal Sinha.

The Sāṁkhyakārikā with Sāṁkhyatattvakaumudī—Gaṅgānātha Jhā.

Hindu Philosophy—Davies.

Positive Sciences of the Hindus—Seal.

Indian Philosophy, Vol. II, Chap. IV—R.K.

History of Indian Philosophy, Vol. I., Chap. VI—D.G.

THE YOGA SYSTEM.

The following works besides those mentioned in Section 26 of the book:—

Patañjali's Yoga Sūtras with the Commentary of Vyāsa and the Gloss of Vācaspati—S.B.E.

Yoga Aphorisms with the Commentary of Bhoja—Rajendralala Mitra.

Yoga as Philosophy and Religion—Dasgupta.

The Yoga System of Patañjali—Woods, Harvard Oriental Series.

Indian Philosophy, Vol. II, Chap. VI—R.K.

History of Indian Philosophy, Vol. I, Chap. VII—D.G.

THE MĪMĀṀSĀ SYSTEM OR THE PŪRVA MĪMĀṀSĀ.

The following works besides those mentioned in Section 28:—

Introduction to Pūrva Mīmāṁsā—P. Sastri.

The Mīmāṁsā Rules of Interpretation—Sirkar.

Karma Mīmāṁsā—Keith.

Prabhākara School of Pūrva Mīmāṁsā—Gaṅgānātha Jhā.

Ślokavārtika—Gaṅgānātha Jhā.

THE UTTARA MĪMĀṀSĀ OR THE VEDĀNTA.

The Vedānta Sūtras with Śaṁkara's Commentary: English Translation by Thibaut—S.B.E.

The Vedānta Siddhāntamuktāvalī—Prakāśānanda: English Translation by Arthur Venice.

The Vedānta Paribhāṣa: English Translation by Venice (in the Pandit).

The System of the Vedānta—Deussen.

Theism in Mediæval India, Lecture VI—Carpenter.

Māṇḍūkya Upaniṣad with Gauḍapāda's Kārikā—Dvivedi.

Bhagavadgīta with Śaṁkara's Commentary—Mahādeva Śāstri.

The Vedāntic Absolute and the Vedāntic Good—P. Narasiṁham (Mind, N. S., 82 and 93).

Six Systems of Indian Philosophy, Chap. IV—Max Müller.

Pañcadaśī—Śrīnivāsa Rao and Kriṣṇaswāmī Iyer.

Indian Philosophy, Vol. II, Chap. VIII—R.K.

History of Indian Philosophy, Vol. I, Chap. X—D.G.

FOR RĀMĀNUJA'S SYSTEM.

Sarvadarśanasaṁgraha, Chap. IV.

Rāmānuja's Commentary on the Vedānta Sūtras: English Translation by Thibaut in S.B.E. and by Raṅgācārya.

Rāmānuja's Commentary on the Bhagavadgītā: English Translation by Govindācārya.

Yatīndramatadīpikā: English Translation by Govindācārya.

Indian Philosophy, Vol. II, Chap. IX—R.K.

For POST-RĀMĀNUJAN PHILOSOPHY.

Sarvadarśanasaṁgraha, Chaps. V and IX.

Mādhava's Commentary on the Bhagavadgītā and Brahma Sūtras: English Translation by Subbā Rāo.

Mahānirvāṇa Tantra—Avalon.

Śakti and Śākta—Avalon.

The Heart of India—Barnett.

Mediæval Theism in India—Carpenter.

Kashmir Śaivism—Chatterji.

Studies in Śaiva Siddhānta—Nallasvāmi Piḷḷai.

Life and Teachings of Śrī Madhva—Padmanābhācārya.

Tiruvāśagam—Pope.

Outlines of Indian Philosophy, Chaps. II and III—Srinivāsa Iyengar.

LIST OF WORKS CONSULTED

Besides others, mostly original texts, the following works have been consulted in the preparation of this book:—

1. The Nyāya Sūtras of Gautama with the Commentary of Vātsyāyana.
2. English Translation of the above by Dr. Gaṅgānātha Jhā.
3. The Tarkabhāṣa of Keśava Miśra.
4. The Tarkasaṁgraha of Annam Bhatta.
5. The Vaiśeṣika Sūtras of Kaṇāda.
6. English Translation of the above by A. E. Gough.
7. Indian Logic and Atomism by A. B. Keith.
8. The Sāṁkhyakārikā of Īśvarakṛṣṇa, with the Sāṁkhyatattvakaumudī of Vācaspati Miśra.
9. English Translation of the above by Dr. Gaṅgānātha Jhā.
10. Hindu Philosophy—John Davies.
11. The Sāṁkhya System—A. B. Keith.
12. The Yoga Sūtras of Patañjali.
13. The Pūrva Mīmāṁsā Sūtras of Jaimini.
14. The Karma Mīmāṁsā—Keith.

15. The Vedānta Sūtras of Bādarāyaṇa, with the Commentaries of Saṁkara and Rāmānuja.
16. English Translation of the above and the Introduction —Thibaut.
17. The Vedānta Siddhāntamuktāvalī of Prakāśānanda.
18. English Translation of the above by Arthur Venice.
19. The Vedānta Sāra of Sadānanda.
20. The Religion and Philosophy of India: The Upaniṣads by Deussen.
21. Philosophy of the Upaniṣads—A. E. Gough.
22. A Constructive Survey of the Upaniṣadic Philosophy—R. D. Ranade.
23. Buddhism—Rhys Davids.
24. Manual of Indian Buddhism—Kern.
25. Sarvadarśanasaṁgraha: English Translation by Cowell and Gough.
26. A History of Pre-Buddhistic Indian Philosophy—B. Barua.
27. The Six Systems of Indian Philosophy—Max Müller.
28. India—What Can It Teach Us?—Max Müller.
29. The History of Indian Literature—Weber.
30. A History of Indian Philosophy—Dasgupta.
31. Indian Philosophy—Radhakrishnan.
32. The Encyclopædia Britannica.
33. The Encyclopædia of Religion and Ethics.

GLOSSARY

(IV)

GLOSSARY OF IMPORTANT TERMS

Abhāva ... 'Non-existence'—one of the seven categories in the Vaiśeṣika Philosophy.

Addhyāsa ... 'Super-imposition'; 'the apparent presentation of the attributes of one thing in another thing,' as, for example, the presentation of the attributes of a snake in a rope, in darkness; or those of a piece of silver in a conch-shell.

Adṛiṣta ... 'Invisible'; the invisible force or power which is supposed to bring about the results of past actions, and is, therefore, the cause of misery or happiness.

Advaita ... 'Non-dual'; the philosophy of Monism, which holds that Brahman—the absolute principle—is the only reality, and all else is either illusion or a manifestation of Brahman. The term is specially applied to Saṁkara's Monism.

Ahaṅkāra ... The principle of egoism and also the sense of self-consciousness—'I-hood.'

Ajñāna ... 'False knowledge'; the knowledge that the individual self is different from the universal self of Brahman, and that there is duality of existence. 'Avidyā' is another term for 'ajñāna.'

Anumāna ... Inference; one of the Instruments of Knowledge recognised in Indian Logic.

Avidyā ... The same as 'añjāna,' explained above.

Avyakta ... The 'unmanifested'; specially applied to the primordial matter which is the cause of the whole physical universe according to the Sāṁkhya System.

Ācārya ... Preceptor; usually a teacher of philosophy and religion.

Ātman ... Soul, spirit or ego; distinguishable as the individual and the universal *ātman* and defined in different ways by the various systems of Indian Philosophy. Usually it is the psychological ego, but it is also the metaphysical principle of existence in the monistic systems of philosophy.

Bādarāyaṇa ... The author of the Vedānta Sūtras.

Bhagavadgītā ... 'The Lord's Song'—originally a part of the Mahābhārata, and supposed to embody the teachings of Lord Kṛiṣṇa as addressed to Arjuna on the battlefield, during the Great War between the Kauravas and the Pāṇḍavas. It is the most popular book among the Hindus, and is appreciated for its philosophy even by others.

Bhaktimārga ... 'The path of devotion,' considered to be one of the ways of obtaining salvation as distinguished from the 'path of knowledge' (*jñānamārga*).

Bodhisattva ... 'Perfect beings'; in Buddhism, the term is applied to those wise beings who are destined to become a 'Buddha' in the course of time.

Brahman ... The absolute universal principle of all reality; the universal ego; the impersonal God.

Brāhmaṇa ... The first and the highest of the four main castes in Hinduism; one belonging to this caste.

Brāhmaṇas ... The name applied to a number of treatises in the Vedic literature, which deal with the application and use of the Vedic hymns for sacrificial purposes.

Brāhmaṇism ... A name applied to orthodox Hinduism as taught by the priestly class—the Brāhmaṇas.

Brāhmoism ... Religion and philosophy as taught by the Brāhmo Samāja, a society founded in Bengal by Rāma Mohana Roy. It represents a reformed type of Hinduism, and its followers, though small in number, constitute one of the most cultured sections of the Indian people.

Bṛihaspati ... The traditional author of a lost work—the Bṛihaspati Sūtras, supposed to be the main basis of the Materialistic School of Indian philosophy.

Buddha ... The founder of Buddhism, called Prince Siddhārtha in his early life, son of a Kṣatriya king—Śuddhodana. He was born at Kapilavastu about 560 B.C.

Buddhi ... 'Intellect'; defined as the faculty of understanding, reflection or discrimination. It is the active principle of consciousness.

Buddhism ... Religion and philosophy as taught by Buddha.

Caitanya ... 'Pure consciousness'; also the name of a teacher who flourished in Bengal, 1485—1583 A.D.

Cārvāka ... A leading exponent of Materialism.

Darśana ... The Saṁskṛit name for philosophy. The various systems are known as the 'darśanas.'

Dravya ... 'Substance,' one of the seven categories.

Dvaita ... 'Dual,' 'dvaitavāda'—the doctrine of dualism which recognises more than one principle of reality.

Gauḍapāda ... One of the teachers of Monism, the precursor of Śaṁkara's Vedānta; flourished about the 8th Century A.D.

Gautama ... The author of the Nyāya Sūtras.

Gautama Buddha Gautama Buddha is the full name of Buddha, the founder of Buddhism.

Guṇa ... 'Attribute' or 'quality'; one of the categories.

Guṇas ... Attributes; specially used to express the three metaphysical attributes of *Sattva*, *Rajas* and *Tamas* (goodness, foulness or passion and darkness) in the Sāṁkhya System.

Hinayānism ... One of the sections of Buddhism; literally, 'the doctrine of the smaller or inferior path,' so called by the other School of Mahāyānism—'the doctrine of the greater or the superior path.' It represents a Realistic school of thought.

Indriya ... 'Organs,' distinguished as the Organs of Sense and the Organs of action, which are five each.

Jaimini ... The author of the Mīmāṁsā Sūtras and the founder of the Pūrva Mīmāṁsā School of Philosophy.

Jainism ... Religion and philosophy as taught by Mahāvīra, a great saint, born about 599 B.C. Jainism is, however, believed to have existed even before Mahāvīra.

Jīva or *Jīvātma*... The individual soul or the principle of life.

Jñānamārga ... 'The path of knowledge,' which is one of the ways of obtaining salvation, as distinguished from 'the path of devotion'—the '*bhaktimārga*.'

Kabīr ... A religious teacher who is known for his devotional poetry and songs.

Kaivalya ... The state of perfection and emancipation characterised by perfect bliss.

Kaṇāda ... The author of the Vaiśeṣika Sūtras and the founder of the Vaiśeṣika System.

Kapila ... The traditional author of the Sāṁkhya Sūtras and the founder of the Sāṁkhya System.

Karman or ***Karma*** 'Action'; the law according to which the agent is bound to enjoy or suffer the fruits of action; it is the cause of bondage.

Kāraṇa ... 'Cause,' which is of several kinds.

Kārya ... 'Effect,' which is supposed to be either different from the cause or identical with it.

Lokāyatikas ... The followers of the Materialistic School, so called as they are supposed to be attached to the world of sense (*loka*).

Lokottaravādins A Buddhistic School of Philosophy.

Madhvācārya ... A teacher of a Vaiṣṇavite School of Philosophy; born about 1197 A.D.

Mādhyamikas ... A School of Nihilists in Buddhism attached to the Mahāyāna Section.

Mahābhārata ... The Epic poem which describes the Great War between the Kauravas and the Pāṇḍavas. The Bhagavadgītā and a few other portions of it are of a philosophical nature.

Mahāyānism ... 'The doctrine of the greater or superior path'; one of the two main sections of Buddhism; it is distinguished from 'Hīnayānism'—'the doctrine of the smaller or inferior path.' It represents an Idealistic school of thought.

Manas ... The organ of attention, which can attend to only one thing at a time. It is usually supposed to be a physical organ of a very subtle nature and has a different significance from the English word 'mind.'

Māyā ... 'Illusion'; in the Vedānta, especially in Śaṁkara's philosophy, a metaphysical supposition which explains the perception of the phenomenal universe, and is the cause of the apparent distinction between universal reality and individual existence. It is defined as something positive although inexplicable.

Mīmāṁsā ... The philosophy of ritualism as expounded by Jaimini in the Pūrva Mīmāṁsā Sūtras.

Mokṣa ... 'Emancipation'; freedom from the bondage of birth and death by the stoppage of the cycle of *Karman* and its fruits.

Mukti ... ... The same as 'Mokṣa.'

Nāma-rūpa ... 'Name and Form'—the former denotes all mental or internal phenomena, and the latter all physical or external phenomena. It is a term peculiar to Buddhism.

Nānaka ... ... Known as Guru Nānaka, a teacher who flourished in Northern India and was the founder of Sikhism.

Nigodas ... ... A name given to souls or 'soul-clusters' with which the smallest conceivable particle of matter is saturated. 'Nigodas' in Jainism are similar to 'monads' in the philosophy of Leibnitz.

Nirvāṇa ... A term used for emancipation or salvation as it is conceived in Buddhism. It denotes a complete cessation of the life of ***karman*** and a reduction to nothingness.

Nyāya ... ... The system of philosophy which has its basis in the Nyāya Sūtras of Gautama, and represents Indian Logic.

Paramātman ... The supreme spirit; God.

Patañjali ... The author of the Yoga Sūtras and also of the Mahābhāṣya, a commentary on Pāṇini's Grammar.

Piṭakas ... A name given to the three oldest sacred books of Buddhism, *viz.*, Vinaya, Sūtra and Abhidharma.

Pradhāna ... In the Sāṁkhya, a name given to the primordial matter which is the fundamental cause of the material universe.

Prakṛiti ... Nature or matter; in the Sāṁkhya, another name for 'pradhāna.'

Pratyakṣa ... Perception; one of the Instruments of Knowledge.

Puruṣa ... A name for soul or spirit, specially used in the Sāṁkhya.

Rajas ... The attribute of passion; one of the three *guṇas* in the Sāṁkhya philosophy.

Rāmānuja ... Also known as Rāmānujācārya, the author of the ***Srībhāṣya*** on the

		Vedānta Sūtras, and the teacher of the modified monism known as the *Viśiṣṭādvaita;* born about 1016 A.D.
Rāmāyaṇa	...	The Epic poem composed by Vālmīki, which relates the life and adventures of Rāma, a king of Oudh.
Ṛigveda	...	The oldest work in the Saṁskṛit literature, and the first of the four Vedas, which form the basis of all Hindu religion and philosophy.
Sam āhi	...	In the Yoga, a state of deep concentration in which all distinctions are lost.
Samavāya	...	Intimate or inherent relation such as exists between the cause and its effect ; one of the seven categories.
Saṁsāra	...	The phenomenal world of change with all that it implies.
Sattva	...	The attribute of 'goodness'—one of the three *guṇas* in the Sāṁkhya.
Sautrāntikas	...	A Realistic school of Buddhism based upon the 'Sūtras.'
Śaṁkara	...	Also known as Śaṁkarācārya—the greatest exponent of the Vedānta Monism, the author of the Śārīrakabhāṣya on the Vedānta Sūtras.
Śāstra	...	A general name given to any systematic treatise on religion, philosophy, arts or science, which has a regulative force, or is looked upon as a work of authority.
Sraddhā	...	Faith.
Srāddha	...	Offerings to the dead; a regular practice among the orthodox Hindus.

Skanhas ... 'The elements of existence' in Buddhism, which represent the mental and the physical constitution of an individual. They are co-extensive with *Nāma-rūpa.*

Sāmānya ... The notion of generality or genus; one of the categories.

Sāṁkhya ... The dualistic system which is supposed to have been founded by Kapila.

Sūtras ... 'Aphorisms,' terse sentences; works composed of such aphorisms as are characteristic of the main works of the various schools of Indian Philosophy and several works on Saṁskṛit grammar.

Tamas ... 'Darkness'—one of the three attributes in the Sāṁkhya System.

Tīrthaṅkara ... A name given to a Jaina saint who is worthy of worship.

Upamāna ... Analogy or Inference by Analogy, one of the Instruments of Knowledge.

Upaniṣads ... Philosophical treatises which form a part of the Vedas, and are the basis of the monistic school of thought.

Upādhi ... 'Condition,' the 'modifying condition' which particularises the universal and makes it appear as a form of the individual; it is the cause of the illusion which introduces plurality into the unity and absoluteness of true reality.

Uttara Mīmāṁsā Another name for the Vedānta, the doctrine of the absoluteness and unity of existence; also the name of the Vedānta Sūtras of Bādarāyaṇa,

Vaibhāṣikas ... A Realistic school in Buddhism attached to the Hīnayāna section. It is based upon the Abhidharma; and denies the authority of the Sūtras altogether.

Vaiśeṣika ... The system of philosophy founded by Kaṇāda. It is so called because 'viśeṣa'—'a distinguishing attribute,' receives special treatment in it.

Vallabhācārya ... The teacher of what has come to be known as Vallabhism, a religious cult which emphasises unconditional devotion to Kṛiṣṇa; born about 1479 A.D.

Vedānta ... A general name given to the monistic philosophy in India, which is mostly based upon the teachings of the Upaniṣads, the Bhagavadgītā and the Vedānta Sūtras of Bādarāyaṇa.

Vedas ... The four main sacred books of the Hindus—Ṛigveda, Yajurveda, Sāmaveda and Atharvaveda. They are supposed to be revealed by God through the sages and form the highest religious authority.

Vijñānavādins ... Idealists; a school of Idealism in Buddhism.

Viśeṣa ... A distinguishing attribute; specific differentia; species; one of the categories.

Viśiṣṭādvaita ... 'Modified Monism'—a name given to the philosophy of Rāmānuja in order to distinguish it from the Monism of Śaṁkarācārya.

Yoga ... The name of the system as taught by Patañjali in the Yoga Sūtras; the practice of concentration.

Yogācāras ... Also called the Vijñānavādins—an Idealistic school of Buddhism which holds that subjective ideas are the only reality.

INDEX

-In the following index the words are arranged in the order of the English alphabet. Saṁskṛit and Pāli technical terms are in italics. Letters with diacritical marks come after the ordinary ones.

SOME OPINIONS ABOUT THE BOOK.

Professor S. Radhakrishnan, M.A., King George V. Professor of Philosophy and Head of the Post-graduate Department in the University of Calcutta, writes :

"Quite a useful introduction for beginners. In a small compass it gives the chief points of Indian Thought."

Professor W. S. Rowlands, B.A. (Oxon), Head of the Department of Philosophy, Nagpur University, says :

" I have read Mr. Jwala Prasad's 'Introduction to Indian Philosophy' in manuscript. I may say that a publication of this kind would be of real value to M.A. students of the Nagpur University, as the History of Indian Philosophy is a compulsory part of the course in Mental and Moral Science . . . I consider that the author has succeeded in comprehending an immense amount of information into very small limits and that he has done so without sacrifice of lucidity. The main outlines stand out clearly, and the detail is grouped effectively round these. I also believe that he has succeeded in raising philosophic issues of the highest and most lasting importance with the result that the contribution of India to the classical problems of thought is set forth clearly."

Professor R. D. Ranade, M.A., Professor of Philosophy and Head of the Philosophy Department in the University of Allahabad, writes in his Foreword to the book :

" Professor Jwala Prasad, M.A., of Robertson College, Jubbulpore, has laid the student-world under deep obligation by writing a concise and trenchant account of Indian Philosophy . . . There are very few concise manuals of Indian Philosophy of this kind. Professor Jwala Prasad has done great service in writing a book which might be regarded as probably the most suitable introduction among these to this difficult subject.

Within the short compass at his disposal, Professor Jwala Prasad has done his work ably. He touches even the most difficult points in these systems, and treats them in a concise manner."